THE SU

Cathy Douglas graduated from Oxford in 1975 and has worked in publishing ever since. She lives in London with her husband and two cats. She says she is a slapdash housekeeper, an erratic cook, highly disorganized and has never made tomato chutney.

# THE SUPERWOMAN TRAP

## and how to get out of it

*Cathy Douglas*

Futura

A Futura Book



First published in Great Britain in 1984 by
Futura Publications, a Division of
Macdonald & Co (Publishers) Ltd
London & Sydney



ISBN 0 7088 2647 4

Printed and bound in Great Britain by
Hazell Watson & Viney Limited,
Member of the BPCC Group,
Aylesbury, Bucks.

Futura Publications
A Division of
Macdonald & CO (Publishers) Ltd
Maxwell House
74 Worship Street
London EC2A 2EN
A BPCC plc Company

# *Contents*

# 1

## *The Trap Closes*

By now everyone can recognize Superwoman at a glance. She is in her mid-thirties (and never gets a day older). She is most often a full-time professional, ideally on the board of a small company, but certainly at senior management level if she works for a larger firm: sometimes she works part-time, either at home or in the office, while she brings up her family. She rarely has a university degree, or if she does, it is in a 'soft' subject – her background is conventional, rather than academic – but has probably worked her way up to management via her excellent, now normally hidden, secretarial qualifications and her outstanding organizational ability. She gets on well with the rest of the staff and is extremely good at her job without making a fuss about it or compromising her distinctive femininity. At home, she tends to have a permanent man, probably a husband, who does something undefined but well-paid and likely to be more creative than conventional unless he's in the Law or the City. They have a labrador or a cat or both, and since she *is* thirty five, usually one or two young children, in which case they have a live-in nanny with car and colour television, and an account at Mothercare. She also has accounts at Harvey Nicholls and Austin Reed Options; she and her husband have a car each, preferably a company one, and the whole family is covered by one or other of their firms' medical insurance scheme. She is an excellent cook, with a freezer full of gourmet concoctions made in batches at the weekend, a store cupboard full of bulk-bought loo-paper and home-made chutney, from her own tomatoes and Elizabeth David's recipes, and a thriving herb garden on her kitchen windowsill. She does a weekly shop at Safeways and a monthly one at the cash-and-carry, but makes sorties to specialist 'little shops' for fresh pasta, real cheese, arcane fruits and excellent meat. She decorated the house herself, either literally, including mixing her own colours and achieving interesting effects by dragging, or to the extent of choosing everything to be delivered by John Lewis and arranging dates with the workmen, and she learned upholstery so she could re-cover the antique chaise-longue in the spare time from her exercise class or after the children are in bed. She is always slim and beautifully groomed – tailored suits during the week, country casuals or poured-on jeans at the weekend – and has her hair cut and re-touched every month. She has never voiced an opinion on feminism, but you know she thinks it's undignified. She has business lunches at all the best restaurants, where she eats prawns and salads, drinks Perrier water, and is on friendly terms with the Maître d': about once a month she and her husband go out to celebrate something, often with another Supercouple, and then only Michelin-starred establishments need apply. She is also very fond of the theatre (though never the National, the Barbican or the Roundhouse – she goes to be entertained), has heard of all the Booker Prize novels but actually buys coffee-table and cookery books and reads Dick Francis and *The Thorn Birds*; watched *Brideshead* and videoed *Life on Earth*; and is not terribly keen on any sport except Wimbledon and après-ski. She reads the features pages of at least one daily newspaper, buys one or two glossy magazines a month, and takes her holidays somewhere far away and hot in January, leaving the children with Granny; in Scotland en famille in the summer.

In short, she is perfect – and completely insufferable.

Superwoman was born by Women's Lib out of the Permissive Sixties, but with a strong genetic inheritance from her homemaking grandmother. The midwives were mostly the new *Cosmopolitan* breed of magazines, supported by the rest of the media and cheered on by the vast majority of women. There were only good fairies at her christening, and they all worked very hard at making her perfect, none more so than her chief godmother Shirley Conran who gave her, as soon as she was old enough to read it, her manual of essential information in steering her way to Superwomanhood.

And, for a time, the spells worked. Superwoman came of age as talented as she was attractive, and her large following of handmaids continued to follow her every step with dedication and enthusiasm. A 'significant number' of women were now occupying top jobs and, especially with the Equal Opportunities Act to open the field to them, many others had given up stuffing mushrooms and jogged their way to join the commuter race. Adverts started showing them beaming their ring of confidence smiles over shorthand pads instead of soapsuds, and selling them perfumes to suit the busy modern woman from morning to midnight. Articles dwelt on the multiple orgasm and the working woman's wardrobe. Progress had been made towards the great goal of woman's realm.

But like all the best christening charms, those given to Superwoman had a sting in the tail. She is after all only an ideal, and a hybrid ideal at that, and so has a right to be perfect. The cracks only start to show when the rest of us try to emulate her perfection, and find it more difficult than we had supposed. Combining motherhood with a career doesn't get noticeably easier, and finding a job at all, let alone a top job, gets considerably harder all the time. Multiple orgasms don't, by and large, happen every day; not everyone can be a Cordon Bleu cook; and no amount of dieting, exercise or make-up can create a model figure that wasn't there to start with.

What really makes Superwoman unbearable is not her perfection, but our own lack of it. She makes us feel guilty for not measuring up, or not having realized there was a competition; we resent her excellence because we feel inadequate for not managing it ourselves, or for not having thought of trying: she's got us both ways round. The image that was born amid such optimism, and as such a laudable attempt to boost our confidence, to show us that we could not only survive but succeed in a world designed for men without losing the more attractive aspects of our femininity, has backfired. She was a necessary invention, and in her day she undoubtedly fulfilled her purpose, but she has simply gone on too long. All the best heroes die young, before their feet of clay start showing: those who survive, like Superwoman, run the risk of turning into tyrants.

If she were real, she would no doubt compound her errors by being kind to children and animals, remembering your birthday, and sending flowers in sickness or in childbirth, and nobody would have a word to say against her – which is the most damning word they could say against anybody. But although it is easy enough to endow Superwoman with characteristics, it is impossible to give her a character, which is what's needed if she is to have the possibility of reality. If you try, you will almost certainly find that you come up with an idealization of yourself, with Superwoman's multi-directional talents added (and possibly your nastier habits edited out): and idealizations are always unlovable. Superwoman is like this because she is created from a series of unconnected parts which never will add up to a completely human whole, and were in fact never meant to. It is only the would-be Superwomen who have tried to see her as one complete person who can do everything superbly, forgetting that a few faults are a vital counterbalance to such intimidating perfection.

Many women, of course, don't make that mistake. Some are pretty nearly Superwomen themselves; others never had any ambition to be, or quickly learned to tailor their aims to their capabilities and ignore Superwoman's more outrageous territorial imperatives; among the youngest adults there are plenty who are far enough away from her to see her in the proper perspective. But there is a sizeable section still, ranging in age roughly from twenty-five to forty (unlike Superwoman, the rest of us *do* get older), who have been brought up with the ideal as our one great white hope and, blinded by its promise, are still struggling towards it with a growing sense of discouragement. For the vanguard, the battle has been long and hard, and the victory seems to take unremitting effort to maintain, but they have at least a fair share of the battle honours. For the second rank, the battle fatigue may be even worse: not only are the vanguard still up ahead, occupying the honours in the form of the top jobs currently available to women and thereby creating a limit to the possible achievement, but that achievement is in any case diminished by not being the trail-blazing first. The first woman coal-miner is an object of admiration; the thirty-first, though she may have fought even harder to get there, is nothing unusual. And so we all plod along unsatisfied, in the wake of Superwoman's bravely fluttering banner, consolidating a general position without a whiff of personal glory. We have sold ourselves into an even worse slavery than before, because this time it's our own fault. And the Superwoman Trap is set.

If it were only a question of finding our feet in the world of work, we wouldn't be much worse off than the male victims of the Rat Race, and only a decade or so behind them. (Ironically enough, the general sixties' disaffection with the rat race, and the consequent yearning for the key of life rather than of the executive washroom, was one of the factors which opened the way for a less stereotyped view of work, and therefore contributed to the ease of Superwoman's birth in the first place.) The extra handicaps of being a woman in the workplace are not in themselves insurmountable – but Superwoman does not confine her efforts to the business world. She conducts her war on every front at once, and is as concerned with creating an attractive home and seducing 'him' with steaks and candlelight as she is with putting one over the opposition in a tricky boardroom deal.

The magazines are a very good example of the contra-directional behaviour of Superwoman. The one which tells us how to be a superbusinesswoman is not necessarily the same one – or at least not the same issue – that tells us how to be a supercook, superbeauty, superdecorator or super-sex-kitten, but the cumulative effect is to leave us feeling guilty and inadequate if we can't cope with all of them at once, or don't want to. Even going to a party gets the heavy treatment from *Look Now*: 'Planning for a party, even if it isn't your own, requires a lot of thought and effort. What shall I wear? Who shall I take? How will I get home? They're all questions a frenzied partygoer asks before the big day. But an organized and veteran partygoer will be thinking about these points within minutes of receiving the invitation . . . Each one, like a battle, needs careful strategy. If you take the attitude that you'll only get out of a celebration what you put in to it, you'll realize that with party-planning, there's actually an awful lot at stake.' (December 1983)

Ye Gods! A battle indeed – and that's even before we get there. No wonder we feel tired all the time. It might be simpler to stay at home with *Cosmopolitan* (Getting High on Work), or *Woman's World* (I Climbed to the Top of the World: One Woman's Adventure), or *Company* (Teach Yourself Popularity), or *Honey* (Are you still his domestic slave?), or any of the other myriads of magazines devoted to showing us so helpfully what we should or could be doing, or worrying about, or improving upon, to make the grade as Superwoman. Or then again, maybe it would be simpler still to crawl away and bury our incompetent carcasses under the labour-saving duvet . . .

Normally, of course, we don't see all these magazines at once and so don't get the overkill effect which makes them funny; it's more like a Chinese water torture, slowly and inexorably dripping away on our self-confidence. We don't have time to read them much, we're too busy trying to obey them all – and that's not easy, when they're capable of such staggering contradictions. *Cosmopolitan* had 'Cheers, you're Single!' and 'Quiz: How good a bet is he?' in the same issue, and they're all quite likely to order us severely to get out there and change our life immediately in the same breath as they sympathize with our stressful existence and urge us to relax – though even this is treated as hard work ('Seasonal Stress: How to Fight Apathy and Find Energy' – *Company*). And rarely does it occur to any of them that we might be quite happy muddling along with our own unsatisfactory lives in our own way.

The contradictions are inherent in Superwoman, and are what makes her so impossible and the Superwoman Trap so inexorable. She exists independently on each front; it is only the would-be Superwoman who tries to combine them all. We are the first generation ever to do so: previously a woman either worked (and then inevitably in a menial position), in which case she was not only not expected to entertain, and look well-groomed, and read fashionable novels, but would have been actively discouraged from doing so; or she was more well-to-do and had servants to run her household, nothing at all to do *except* look delightful, entertain marvellously, keep up with cultural affairs and perhaps operate some mild charity work, and wouldn't only not be equipped to work properly but would get some very odd comments if she tried it. Whether you credit it to the easier social mobility of the working classes or the financially necessary greater social acceptability of work itself of course it's an improvement and an emancipation to have a choice – but a straight merger is going a bit far. Yet every time we see one of those top-grade Superwoman acolytes who does seem to have managed it profiled – in between the instructional articles – our competitive instincts are aroused, and we know that we're letting the side down if we don't follow suit. We apply ourselves once more to the long, hard road, and while everyone around us seems intent on filling the unforgiving minute (ours) with ninety minutes worth of distance run, we know it's for our own good. They're right. It takes effort to become a Superwoman – and we don't stop to consider that we usually stay exactly on the same spot at the end of it.

One of our problems is that in many ways it genuinely *is*

right. Equality of the sexes is still far from a reality, and until it is the effort is necessary. A sensible article on 'Success and the Men in your Life' concluded: 'As you are the pioneering generation of working women who are going out and doing it, then it's bound to be tough. But only by your example can the next generation of men and women grow up thinking it natural that everybody has the right to do what they want.' (Paul Kerton, *Company*, March 1984). The subject was actually friction between the sexes in careerism, but the principle holds even better in the larger context of the complete Superwoman lifestyle. It seems – *is* – right, and it sounds reasonable: until it occurs to you that you didn't actually choose to become an early Christian martyr. The choice was forced on you by the changing shape of a world which made your enlistment both a social and usually an economic necessity.

Another problem with Superwoman is that before she discovered her true potential as a company director, she was brought up to believe in the good old-fashioned virtues of homemaking, attracting men, and then bearing and bringing up their children while being supportive of their careers. When career prospects came along for her as well she embraced them warmly, and would in fact be inconceivable without her working life, either present or past; but she still wants to get married and have children, and at heart is really a domestic person. When she first came into being there seemed to be an unspoken assumption that the problems of work stopped the moment you stepped outside your front door on your way there: you worked, but the work itself was a shadowy, docile thing, creating no worries apart from how to take eight hours out of the twenty-four and still find time to talk to the children, cook 'his' supper, and clean the windows. Shirley Conran devoted a mere eleven pages to 'How to be a Working Wife and Mother', as against fifteen on 'How to be a Housemaid' and twenty on 'Food'. Since then, of course, the world has moved on, and our ambitions and aspirations for our career stretch rather further: but while this has been reflected by the increase in coverage of work ethics and self-improvement, there has still been no corresponding decrease in the standards set for our cooking, our interior design, our motherhood, our figures, or our perennial search for a perfect husband.

It's a very rare daughter who doesn't crave, however subliminally, her mother's approval, and these homemaking ideals belonged to Superwoman's mother as well as to yours, and to hers, and so on back through thousands of years of social evolution. So it is hardly surprising that Superwoman has adopted them, or that we are automatically inclined to hold them in respect. And thus Superwoman nearly always has a husband and children; so the assumption about men is always that the search is for a permanent relationship, and the articles about being swinging and single always have a rallying tone, as if singles need special encouragement; so features on health, beautiful bathrooms, souper soups and preparing for parties will always take up more column inches than those on how to get up the company ladder.

Of course it would be ridiculous to sit back and simply blame the power of the media for creating the Superwoman Trap. These magazines and papers and programmes were instituted, like any successful business, on the basis of exhaustive market research, and judging from their healthy variety – and their circulation figures – the answers they came up with were pretty well on target. If they initially showed us the glory that was Superwoman, we were eager to look, and after that first marriage of true minds who led whom on is immaterial. We could equally well blame our mothers, for the demands made by their conditioning, or men, for the demands made by theirs; or the feminist movement, for the revolutionary stand it had to take to gain any ground at all; or whole generations of women for creating a reputation for our sex as good managers. They are all contributory factors, but none of them could have done it alone: they just happened to coincide with each other and us in a period of social flux. And in any case, if you've got thoroughly enough into the Superwoman Trap you won't be content with any scapegoat but yourself – which certainly won't serve any useful purpose in getting you out of it.

If you *are* in the trap, you will almost certainly recognize it already, or be too busy running to catch up with yourself to stop and think about it. You will be overworking for your salary – to a point which even you recognize as overwork – and overworking every evening and all weekend trying to run your home as if that was your full-time job too. If you aren't going out to work, you will either be fretting to get back to it, or throwing yourself into domesticity with a vengeance, whether to convince yourself of how rewarding it is, or to end up with a showhouse, a show-garden, and prize-winning tomato chutney. Either way, you will fight off the occasional ignoble spurt of rebellion and slog away at your effort to become something you're never going to achieve and probably don't even want to be. Slowly but surely, you lose your capacity for relaxation, and even for doing those Superwomanlike things you used to do, like playing squash, or having dinner parties, or booking a summer holiday. You begin to resent those who aren't as trapped as you are: first those who have – or make – more leisure for themselves (you think they're not pulling their weight), then those who even dare enjoy themselves (don't they realize how important it is?). Complaining about your lot – but in such a way as to make it clear that it's only tough because you're so good at everything you're indispensable – becomes a permanent habit, and worse still you can hear yourself whining and dislike yourself for it. You don't have time to take your full holidays from the office, or a day out from home. You're too tired to cook. You meet your fellow-victims in winebars and talk wistfully of living in a cottage with roses round the door and breeding goats, though in your heart you know you'd be bored silly in a month and anyway suspect you mightn't even like it. You become obsessed with material standards. Your social life – apart from the goat breeding sessions – disintegrates, because you can't cope with having people round, or are too tired to go out. You get run down and depressed (all those winebars and not cooking) but 'can't afford' to take a healing day in bed, so you slow up, and then work even harder to try and recoup. You are firmly in the Superwoman Trap, and there doesn't seem to be any way out.

It sounds facile, but the trap can have quite serious consequences – the least tangible but most universal of which is that there is a largish group of unhappy women making their own and other people's lives a misery. The constant effort, especially since it's in conflicting directions, can very easily lead to stress, which is a fully-paid-up medical condition and is known to be on the increase, particularly among women, and even more particularly among women managers. And if the trap's effects become widespread, it could even have a detrimental effect on equality in the workplace – because if after only a dozen or so years of partial equality there, women can reach a level of stress not normally achieved by men for twice that time-span, then the one thing our employers are *not* going to do is congratulate us on our rapid progress . . .

One of the really insidious dangers of the trap is that its chief effect is the guilt which makes us rush further into its grip. A thorough-going Trap-ee will find whole booksful of excellent excuses for continuing her ruinous behaviour; working late at the office, pushing herself unmercifully at the chores, flinging herself into an orgy of motherhood (especially if she has left the child with a nanny during the day), and cramming for her evening class as though it were a D.Phil course. Usually she will earnestly reassure remonstrators that she knows it's ridiculous but it's all right, things will calm down when the presentation is over, or the nanny's settled in, or whatever. And disentangling yourself, when you are so determinedly becoming further entangled all the time and are moreover so unhappily certain that you deserve to suffer not only for the good of future generations but largely because of your own failures, is obviously not going to be easy.

The trap affects all aspects of our lives, creeping outwards from the vital preoccupations of work, home and motherhood, through relations with both the men and the women in our lives, to the point where even gaining two pounds, stalling the car, or oversalting the potatoes can assume the catastrophic proportions of Custer's Last Stand. Some aspects are clearly more closely enmeshed than others – everyone has some sort of home, one must eat, and one can't exclude human interreactions from anything, while the style of our work and our motherhood or lack of it will both determine the structure of our whole life. So that although the following chapters will look at each area in turn some will overlap, or take a different angle on the same subject; and none of them will offer a perfect blueprint for your individual situation, or a universal cure-all for anything. Their purpose is rather to explain some of the major manifestations of the trap, and some of the reasons for them, on the principle that knowledge is an even better form of defence than attack is, and ridicule is the best of the lot.

Despite the fact that everybody has a home, it is in the nature of the beast that every Superwoman's spiritual home is in an office, and that is then the logical place to start: which makes the next chapter recommended reading for the morning train-ride . . .

# 2
## *A Woman's Work*

Superwoman can, of course, flourish in other working environments such as schools, hospitals, shops and probably almost any other you care to name, but her natural habitat is that main arena of careerism, the office. Only here can she find the wealth and variety of stimuli to Superwomanhood in their most concentrated form, though it goes without saying that the basic principles of Oneupwomanship in the office also apply to all other types of paid work. Equally and conversely, not every woman in an office has aspirations to be a Superwoman at all, but will almost certainly recognize those of her colleagues who do.

The working would-be Superwoman is easily spotted. She arrives at eight, because she has so much to do; or at ten, because the car broke down, the cat was sick, the alarm didn't go off or she was dropping in the dry-cleaning. She is usually wearing a suit – although there are days when she doesn't look quite as efficiently tailored as she would like; she's been too hectic at work to keep up with the laundry at home, and anyway she can't rid herself of the habit of impractical impulse buys, which makes her wardrobe somewhat inconsistent; she may not have got round to make-up either. Her executive slim-line briefcase is distorted through constant overfilling, and is supplemented by a bulging carrier bag of paperwork. Her office is a total chaos of paper, overflowing from every filing tray all over the desk and often on to the floor and windowsills, and interspersed with dry-cleaning tickets, birthday cards, left-behind sweaters and aspirin packets, and her sole contribution to botany is a dead African violet. Her harassed secretary alternates between bouts of frenzied activity, and utter boredom, because there never seems to be time to delegate or explain; the one thing she can be certain of is that the urgent document which needs five pages of typing and thirty sets of photocopies won't materialize on her desk until 5.29 p.m. Despite this, she is generally popular with her staff, who are frequently maddened by her but tend to be amazingly tolerant and understanding of her vagaries: she, for her part, spends a lot of time feeling guiltily apologetic towards them, and the rest of it pushing them as hard as she pushes herself. They are mostly women – the would-be Superwoman hasn't quite mastered the art of giving direct instructions to men, though she deals with them happily on an interdepartmental basis: friction is always more likely to occur with other women, but so are appointments under her. Her colleagues of both sexes come to her with all their fiddliest and most time-consuming problems, which she deals with a lot more efficiently than she ever does with her own – except that she sometimes shows a tendency to snap or sigh at them, and gets impatient when they pause for a chat or a joke. She goes to meetings with a huge pile of files which are rarely useful, either because the information is in her head anyway or because it is still in her in-tray; she is almost impossible to reach by phone, as she automatically puts off taking the call until the current crisis is over. Unfortunately this failing often causes routine jobs to develop into crises through neglect, a state of affairs exacerbated by her constant panic level blurring her priorities. She either works through lunch; or gets so tired she goes down to the pub at ten to two for congealing sausage and mash; or rushes frenetically round town buying food for supper, paying the gas bill (on final demand), collecting the cleaning and grabbing the only sandwich left – cheese and tomato on white – to eat on her way back. She hates business lunches, because she never feels she has the time to spare, and can't really believe that such a leisured and apparently purposeless occasion can be work, yet she might easily spend an hour on the phone sorting out some problem with the nanny or the builders that could perfectly well wait until the evening. She doesn't talk about holidays until June, when she suddenly finds that everyone else has got in first and she can't go until October; she hasn't taken her full allocation in years. She never *ever* leaves work on time unless she has to get back to the children, and will even apologize for going before six on the rare occasions she does so: she claims she can get through masses of work when the office is empty and the phones have stopped ringing, but in practice she tends to be pottering about fairly unproductively. When she does get home she is always tired, frustrated and depressed, because despite her enormous expenditure of energy and woman-hours she doesn't actually seem to have got much *done*.

Of course not all would-be Superwomen do all these things – it's like one of those quizzes where 'if you answered yes to more than three questions . . .' – and of course there are always different degrees of behaviour as well. But the overall picture is a very long way from the cool, efficient image of Superwoman, or from our real-life role models of the current Businesswoman of the Year nominees. So how did the reality diverge so far from the dream?

For a start, the dream was based on Superwoman's one-dimensional nature, so that it ignores the interplay of committees with cooking, bedmaking with board meetings, chicken-pox with conferences. It then teleported Superwoman into her job from space, without taking into account any of the difficult and confusing travel systems the rest of us have to use to get to ours, and from there on it proceeded as if everything related to work was equal between the sexes. Unfortunately, that simply isn't true.

Sex discrimination itself is not the subject of this book, but it is nevertheless an important factor in the extra stresses facing women at work, right from the moment they first begin to look for a job. Despite the Equal Opportunities Act, the sheer biological fact of being female is still seen as a disadvantage that must be outweighed by commensurately higher advantages in the form of job experience, qualifications, or a cracking good figure. It is still possible for a firm to reject a woman applicant because 'we've had trouble with them before': inconceivable that this could be said of a man, though employment statistics alone make it certain that they have been *much* more trouble. Young women – in other words, all those with the education and aspirations to be in a position for equal competition – 'will only leave to get married', unless they already are married, in which case 'they won't be giving 100 per cent to their work'. Then there is always that splendid, and by no means rare, get-out clause for when a woman is otherwise unfaultably suitable, about 'personality problems', a vague but obviously quite terrible phenomenon which apparently only afflicts women, and which has in fact been cited against the candidate not by a man, but by another woman, each time I've heard it used.

Men, having kept work as their exclusive preserve for so long, *are* defensive with the women who try to enter it, and show a strong tendency to shunt us into the more traditional female roles – not managing director, but his PA; not headmaster, but deputy; not sales, but personnel, and so on. The announcement of a woman's appointment to a mainstream job is frequently accompanied by the excuse that she is in some way exceptional: we have no right, as men do, to be merely usefully mediocre, as this wouldn't justify the dangerous step of admitting us to their ranks. (Yet a lawyer acquaintance complained recently 'The trouble with women lawyers is that they're all so darned *clever* . . .')

On the plus side, however, women do have the advantage in the job market of being cheaper to employ. A recent report on male-female differences in the ILEA 'threw up a surprise finding that women in quite senior and responsible posts were often on a lower salary grade than male counterparts' (David Shaw, the *Standard*

19.1.84). A surprise? Perhaps, to the average nice, fair-minded, uncynical man, who is probably sublimely unaware of his own inbuilt advantages and would be shocked if he knew the half of them; but I suspect to very few women. It is a simple statistical truth that women across the board are paid less than men for doing the same job: the level of hierarchy which sets salaries almost certainly consists largely of the older, less broadminded men; and women are in any case notoriously bad at setting a high enough value on themselves.

And even once you've got the job, the problems haven't stopped. There are a number of comparative lists going the rounds at the moment, differentiating the attitudes to men and women – he knows what he wants, she's pushy; he has a great eye for detail, she nit-picks, that sort of thing – and although they are inevitably rather crudely exaggerated they have their basis in truth. Even where sex discrimination no longer exists overtly – which means among the vast majority of men as well as women – it has left its legacy in a whole array of confused attitudes, assumptions and expectations. The effect is strongest among women: because we have been conditioned to expect discriminatory attitudes from our male colleagues, we will tend to see them even where they don't exist, and quite possibly succeed in creating barriers that needn't be there. Add to that our awareness of the discrimination that *is* there, and it is hardly surprising that women cannot yet settle down to believe in their own equality as a given factor, not something that needs constant reinforcement. And until we can, we can hardly expect men to, so we end up with neither sex completely comfortable with each other, and women in particular bringing an over-awareness of our femininity into the most irrelevant equations.

Men have their problems with work too, of course they do; most of them are well-documented under the general heading of the Rat Race, though a few are caused by the female invasion. The urge towards overwork, for example, is no respecter of sex, and nor is the bloody-minded photocopier that always chooses exactly the wrong moment to go into a massive sulky silence. But there are four main areas where the would-be Superwoman, who, like her male rodent counterpart, is ambitious and highly-motivated towards success, works under added disadvantages: in attitude, facilities, peripheral activity, and home affairs.

Firstly, both her own and her colleagues' attitude to her job have been coloured by that congratulatory letter which arrived with her contract, saying how pleased the company is to have attracted such an exceptional employee (the excuse they gave themselves for performing the revolutionary step of appointing her): not only is she going to have to live up to this reputation, but she can be fairly sure that rumours of it have ensured that her colleagues are waiting in gleeful anticipation for a sight of her feet of clay. She is also acutely conscious that she owes it not only to herself but to future generations of women to excel: she is the role model for those who come after her as surely as her forerunners were role models for her, so that the twin pressures of emulation and example will make her set her target not far short of perfection. And it is not simply her ability at the actual work that will be judged. She has got to prove – or thinks she's got to – that she can fall into step without causing an upheaval in the male ranks; and at the same time she mustn't sacrifice either her femininity or her intelligence in order to achieve this end. She has read the articles about self-confidence, and knows she must tread a fine line between assurance and aggression; her looks will be watched as closely as her work is, and she must decide whether she wants a reputation as a flirt (she talks to men), a gossip (she talks to women), or stand-offish (she gets on with her job and keeps her head down). In all these respects her severest critics will almost certainly be women, and it will be very hard for her to come to terms with the realization that her supposed sisters-in-arms are more likely to resent than welcome her. For those who have rejected Superwomanhood in favour of a cushy number (and there are plenty in every office) she poses a threat in that her work is liable to show up their deficiencies; the would-be Superwomen ahead of her are frequently afflicted by an absurd paranoia about competition from their female juniors, and a determination to 'keep them in their place'. This hostility among the reportedly friendly natives is perhaps the biggest single blow facing her, and to learn your way around it is very much harder than to learn the appropriate line to take with men, because it undermines everything you have read or supposed about the solidarity of the sisterhood.

Women, especially ambitious ones, are generally much less tolerant than men are, both of themselves and of others, and the would-be Superwoman will risk making herself unpopular by reacting sharply to errors, laziness or thoughtlessness. She lacks both the easy acceptance and the self-confidence that brings it which men have, and will suffer secretly if she doesn't get constant reassurance of her own ability, likeability, and the purity of her colleagues' motives in any dissent (is it a plot to undermine her?). Her heightened self-awareness may be a largely self-created problem, but it can be real and severe, and a major contributory factor to the stress of her position.

It is extremely hard to clarify all the finer shades of attitude that come into the equation: much easier to evaluate are 'facilities' – apart from their unfortunate tendency to get mixed up with status. Most of them centre on clerical or secretarial work. Our would-be Superwoman is no snob, and will turn her hand to anything as and when the need arises, but she *is* being paid to be a manager: yet an obstinate belief persists that all women can type while no man can, and that even if she is being paid twice a secretarial salary a female manager will happily waste her skills and the company's money for them by doing all her own typing and filing. Men, who are no fools, encourage this illusion by hollering for help at the drop of a company report – and usually get it; women do nothing to dispel it, rushing in to display our competence where angels fear to show a halo-tip, and are consequently expected to show a 100wpm dexterity at least in emergencies. (I, who never got beyond my first typing lesson, once found myself slaving late at night over a complicated document on behalf of a helpless male colleague, only to discover weeks later that he was a proficient touch-typist who wisely kept his skills for his football club activities, safely away from the office.) And it is extraordinarily galling to be greeted with roars of laughter when we request a decent typewriter, whoever's going to use it: sometimes it can seem as if an endless procession of gleaming black all-singing, all-dancing, electronic machines are passing before our eyes into other people's offices as we thump sullenly away at the veteran Imperial with an out-of-alignment 'e' and no key for the pound sign.

I suppose it isn't terribly surprising: we've already agreed that Superwoman probably started her career as a Supersecretary, and non-typing female managers do still seem to be the exception rather than the rule. Particularly when you've been promoted within the same company, you may well find it tricky to explain to the hard-pressed personnel officer, who gets asked for at least three new secretarial posts a day and can only afford one a year, that although, yes, you do know how to type, you're not actually being paid to do it any more; no, you aren't getting above yourself, but it's just that someone has got to do that job so you can deal with your new responsibilities. And for 'secretary' you can read 'assistant' or 'deputy', and so on all the way up. And women themselves find it much harder to draw a lateral cut-off line between themselves and the vacuum below them – perhaps because they are unused to and distrustful of the old-style hierarchies, and quite right too, but it doesn't do much to help anyone else draw it either.

We will also be behind our male counterparts in the queue for an office, a company car, a direct telephone line. That sounds for a moment like status-ridden jealousy, and of course it isn't true of all men in all organizations, or even of all the men in your organization – just prevalent. But suppose for a moment that your job is identical with his as far as job descriptions are concerned. Then imagine he has all these facilities, plus a secretary with the brand-new typewriter, and that you have none of them. Now, assuming they are all provided for genuine job efficiency and not just as perks, it shouldn't take you long to work out the sort of handicap under which you're trying to compete. I suppose you *could* always take it as an enormous compliment, but I wouldn't have the nerve to suggest it.

To many men, and possibly to even more of the first-rank Superwomen who had to work so much harder to get them, these facilities *are* all direct marks of status, and the very fact that somebody hasn't got them places that person, in their minds, a step down in the hierarchy – and causes a seething cauldron of resentment if they then acquire them without attendant promotion. This partly explains why we are so unsuccessful in gaining facilities: being new to the rules of office hierarchies, we didn't demand them as an inalienable condition of our employment, but only asked for them later when we discovered they were necessary to the job. We can therefore be seen to be status-jumping and trying to erode a fragile cobweb of differentials, which of course can't be allowed. It may seem blindingly obvious to you that you want them to increase output, not to give you Brownie points, but to your opponent that's feminine logic and shows you don't understand the complex set of priorities operating at top level – and that should put you in your place!

These difficulties with facilities would probably be well on their way to disappearing by now if it weren't for the general, unshakeable belief that women will 'manage'. We've spent centuries priding ourselves on it, we've convinced both men and ourselves that it's true, and we'll cut our own throats by proving it. (I did once get an assistant – temporarily – by making three major errors in as many weeks, but I didn't do it on purpose and I wouldn't recommend it as a general policy.) We're going to be Superwomen, remember? Which means that a simple little thing like knocking up a ten-page report for the Chairman overnight, even if we do have to use the old Imperial, shouldn't be beyond us, should it? We will still produce accurate accounts or wonderfully creative copy amid the sound and fury of an open plan office, won't we, girls? We will fit in that vital phone call to our top client between the filing clerk's social arrangements and our colleagues' equally vital calls to their clients. We will get up two hours earlier to struggle up to Bradford on the train for that important conference, lugging a huge case of company literature (which we wouldn't dream of feebly asking a man to carry for us) and with our supposedly uncrushable evening dress scrumpled into our handbag, and when we get there only five minutes late we will endure the banter about female unpunctuality with a smile. And we will do it all better, faster, and more calmly than anyone else. Women are the coping sex, and somehow we *will* cope; what's more, we'll be daft enough to boast about it. Can you blame anyone for taking advantage of such a willing victim? Well all right, but not *entirely*.

If uncertainties of attitude affect all working women, and the facilities fallacy also affects some men, the field of 'peripheral activity' troubles nobody but the would-be Superwoman. It is here that the trap really begins to bite, where you can most easily find yourself inextricably caught without having the faintest idea how it happened.

Look around any office, and you will find that all those nice, neatly-boxed job descriptions don't butt tidily together but are fringed by a misty grey sort of no-man's-land. Whose job is it to fill the communal kettle? Repair or report the temperamental photocopier? Answer colleagues' phones when they're away from their desks, or cover for them while they're on holiday – and *know* which messages need immediate action? Know where to find the key to the stationery cupboard after hours? Explain to the new boy in Forward Planning where to find the files he's looking for? Take notes during the three-hour meeting at the end of which the Chairman's going to say, 'Somebody let me have the minutes first thing tomorrow'? Change a typewriter ribbon late at night? Remind Order Processing that their figures will be needed on Monday, because they certainly won't remember for themselves? Know that the Finance Director's secretary is upset over a row with her boyfriend? Make sure there isn't a sudden dearth of folders just before the major conference, like there was last year? Organize the collection for Fred's leaving present?

I needn't go on: you know as well as I do it's a woman. We aren't nearly as good as men are at approaching our job in isolation from the whole – or, to put it another way, we're a lot better at seeing the complete picture. A man will be as good, and often better, at sympathizing with his own junior's family problems, but he won't even have a clue that the plump fair-haired girl on the second floor has any. He will work till the cows come home to do what's required specifically of him, but only a woman will organize the details that nobody remembered to mention. Women are less departmentalized, with more of the housemother instinct: to a would-be Superwoman, every problem is her problem, every failing in some way reflecting on her.

This doesn't mean that the permanent fuzz of trivia doesn't have to be dealt with, or that anyone else *will* remember. But if you touch anything in that peripheral grey area – and it does seem so childish not to when it needs to be done – it has a nasty habit of attaching itself, burr-like, to your existing responsibilities, both in everyone else's mind and in your own. And after that it's only a matter of time until every knotty problem, every piece of bumf that nobody quite knows what to do with, every abnormal extra workload, is firmly wriggling its way into your in-tray crying 'You did me *last* time!' or 'I'm the sort of thing you're so *good* at!' – and there you are, lumbered.

Last of the four, but by no means least, is the near-total inability of women to keep the various segments of our lives in different pigeon-holes. This extraordinary capacity also seems to be starting to disappear among the younger men, but they lack the sense of guilt imparted to us by Superwoman's other, homemaking, facets. Even if you are single, you will worry about your standards of housewifery, and may worry about 'letting yourself go' if you don't solemnly cook at least a couple of times a week rather than eating beans on toast. If you live with a man, an extra element of guilt creeps in, mixed with your early conditioning: he will feel threatened and neglected unless you pay him at least as much attention as you pay your job. If you have children, the guilt is greatest of all: here you are, leaving the baby in its formative years, when the stimulus of your presence could be vital to its wellbeing and development. And yet you must go to that meeting/finish that paperwork/see that client . . .

Seriously, the conflicts between Superwoman as earth-mother and Superwoman as career girl are by no means easily dealt with. Many a working woman has, jokingly exasperated, exclaimed 'What I need is a wife!', and even if she's single it is frequently true. Her position is at best difficult, at worst intolerable, and always a tightrope, with guilt lurking on either side. Because of Superwoman's celebrated homemaking abilities, she may guiltily brush aside the very idea of a home help, even if she can afford one. If she has a partner, the automatic belief in her duty to him is very strong, and his may, depending on his upbringing, be even stronger. But for a working woman with children and, usually, a husband, the contradictory senses of duty and desire are in constant warfare. Not only is her working life made much more difficult initially by the reams of paperwork surrounding maternity leave; not only does the process of pregnancy and childbirth cause emotional and practical upheavals that can take much longer to resolve than the statutory four months; but even if she weathers those storms successfully she then faces a wearing and usually unrecognized campaign to reconcile the two apparently irreconcilable facets of her nature. She loves her job, which would if allowed to take up 90 per cent of her time: she loves her child, which would do the same. And from a purely practical point of view, she must be prepared to drop everything and run in the face of unforeseen disasters at home, while to maintain her job satisfactorily she must be able to forget her personal life for its imperatives.

In any of these three states, you will be subjected to pressure above and beyond the call of your job description – oh, in graduating order of severity, but always there, and at the same time as the pressure from within the office. Still, somehow you are keeping abreast of your own business, as well as minding the dregs of everyone else's; in fact, there are times when you wonder resentfully why they employ anyone else in the wretched place. You're obviously indispensable. Your superiors keep telling you you're wonderful (especially when they explain why you can't have a rise, or a new typewriter). You must be Superwoman, which is what you always wanted.

Well, yes, but . . . Surely Superwoman doesn't get so tired all the time? Surely she doesn't work a ten-hour day and hit the gin bottle when she gets home, or search for hours through three-weeks-worth of in-tray for the letter she knows is in there somewhere? Surely she has people to delegate things to, and an office where she can occasionally get some peace and quiet? Surely, in *her* company, the photocopier works, and people don't ask for major projects at twenty-four hours notice? Surely she doesn't feel irritated by little things like that anyway? And above all, surely she doesn't feel constantly on the edge of panic, as if she's running to catch up with the rest of the world all the time? Surely she's *happy*? So what on earth's gone wrong with you?

The answer is of course that nothing at all has gone wrong with you – just with her. There may be some managerial jobs that can be done properly by one person during the statutory working hours, but according to my friends they are not to be found in banking, local government, journalism, accountancy, the law, publishing, teaching, medicine, retail management, travel or computers – or if they are, not in *their* firm/branch/school/ hospital. And if they're right, even allowing for the fact that they, like you, are probably running the place in their spare time as well, then it's not surprising you're tired. And irritable. And yearning miserably for that cottage with the roses round the door. But Superwoman is obviously living in Cloud Cuckoo Land. So what are you going to do about it?

I'm assuming that you do want to carry on working at a stimulating job you're good at – or to get one – and aren't really going to chuck it all in for a rich husband or goat-breeding, either of which would get you nicely out of the work trap but might be a case of frying pans and fires. In which case, something has certainly got to be done about you. You might even feel better already, because it does look a bit silly, all that anguish, when it's down in black-and-white, doesn't it? And it might be encouraging to know you're not the only mug out there. (On the other hand, you might think I've got it all wrong, it's too facile, and nobody understands just how complicated your problems are, in which case I'm sorry to have to tell you that you're a very typical Trap-ee.) But beyond that superficial reassurance that there never was a bowl of cherries, only pits, I can only offer you two sorts of advice, the philosophical and the practical, and be reasonably sure that you'll find lots of very good reasons for not taking any of it.

The philosophical advice is both the harder, because it means reappraising the way you think, and the easier, because you can't produce hard and fast evidence for why it won't work in your particular case. First of all, dig out your contract from the back of your desk drawer and read it, making sure that you are absolutely clear in your own mind what your working hours and holiday entitlement are supposed to be and what your sickness benefits allow you. Now consider what you think of your employer.

Does the company have a reputation for altruism, or for falling over backwards to be generous to its staff? No? Then why do you suppose they are allowing you, in this uncharacteristically open-handed fashion, to take four weeks holiday a year? Why do you suppose they organize sickness benefits? Why do you suppose, too, successive governments have placed a statutory limit on the number of hours you work a week? Out of liberal idealism? To keep down unemployment? Something to do with Lord Shaftesbury?

Of course not. Both of them are moved by one consideration chiefly, and that is efficiency. You, in other words, are doing nobody any favours by nobly coming in with a streaming cold, forfeiting a quarter of your holiday allowance or working ten hours a day without breaking for lunch. Those times and breaks are laid down because people work better when they aren't overtired, and you won't be at all popular when you give a third of the office your cold. Just look at it from the company's point of view – they may have looked to you like benefits and entitlements, but at the same time they are simply sound business practice. 'Aha,' you say, 'but in my firm you get an extra day's holiday when you've been there thirty years, or if you're a director – that proves it's a perk.' Well, partly. But has it occurred to you that you're also much more likely to get stale after thirty years in one place, or that the level of pressure on the board members might even be greater than it is on you? You'll normally be the first to deny that anything is offered for free: accept that in this instance you're absolutely right, and just remember it when you wake up with a temperature of 103°, decide to work through lunch, or sacrifice your holiday to the sales conference.

With this novel idea in mind, look at your job description, and consider whether it is probable, in a period of recession, that any employer is going to create or perpetuate a job that takes up less time than the span allotted for its performance. Unlikely, isn't it? Then ask yourself whether you are covering all the points in yours, and before you get struck down with a severe attack of guilt, count up the number of functions you *are* performing which aren't in your job description. Yes, yes, I *know* they've got to be done: for the moment don't worry about anything except to sort them out in your head, so that when you do anything you are absolutely clear about whether it's actually your responsibility or not.

But what if you are totally clued-up about the firm's motives in lavishing these apparent benefits on you, yet still feel you can't take advantage of them because 'nobody else' does, and therefore to remain in contention you've got to sacrifice your health and relaxation the same way as they do theirs? This is where you have to be very objective about the whole thing and tell yourself firmly that, firstly, just because other people are behaving in a stupidly self-destructive fashion is no reason for you to do the same and, secondly, that their job is not the same as yours (no job ever is) and so it would be foolish to make direct comparisons. And you might stop to think how little thanks anyone, including you, gives them for their self-sacrifice – you're much more likely to complain about the germs they're spreading around the office, or make snide comments about their being too inefficient to cover their allotted span of work in the normal time, or secretly regard their ostentatious croaking as more a cry for sympathy than a genuine self-sacrifice at all: and just wonder, mildly, whether others among your colleagues are thinking the same ignoble thoughts about you . . .

Now that you're straight about when you're supposed to be working and what you're supposed to be doing, here's another paradox. It is possible to achieve less by working longer. Not simply because the work-rate slows down – that, as a simple graph, wouldn't show any effect for ages – but more because it's like gradually running down a battery, so that each time you start your engine up again there's a bit less power in it for next time, because you're not recharging it adequately in between. There is also a contributory factor, in that after a while you lose sight of the purpose and priorities of your work, and all that seems important is the amount of time it takes up: inevitably, time becomes less useful the less selective you are about what you put in it. And because so much of your time is spent working, the distinctions between work and free time can become blurred, so that you may actually spend less time working than you would if you spent fewer hours in the office. Again, just remember that next time the cleaner arrives to vacuum around you.

Next, think about the people you work with. Business is supposed to thrive on intercommunication, and from a personal point of view an easy relationship with your colleagues can smoothe the corners of your working life. So it may be worth considering, when you're flying around the office demanding this design, that update and the other invoice all by yesterday, that one doesn't have to be the local gossip to spend a few minutes chatting once in a while – just a good psychologist. You may find, if you'll admit it, that you're being unnecessarily censorious of others, tough on yourself, and generally not the easiest person in the world to work with.

Now look specifically at the men you – and the office rumours – think are good at their jobs and in line for promotion. Men don't have to be 'the natural bosses' to have a few things very well worked out, and just because they *aren't* natural bosses by right of sex doesn't mean necessarily that they're all drones. So do a mental review of what time they arrive, and leave. Do they normally skip lunch? Does their work suffer because they leave the occasional memo for the morning? Does anyone think of blaming them for an oversight of someone else's they didn't pick up, or they of blaming themselves? What's sauce for the gander is sauce for the goose, and you might remind yourself that men still get promoted faster and further than women – so it might be worth trying their style. Even if you cynically believe that all of them survive only through the efficiency of the – junior – women around them, do you have to join the ranks of the nappy-changers?

And talking of nappy-changers, few employers nowadays see themselves as either paternalists or social workers, but they do see it as important to their own efficiency and profitability that their employees should not be overburdened by home problems, and that they should keep experienced personnel wherever they can. Compassionate leave has come a long way since Bob Cratchitt's day, and although maternity leave still has a long way to come, the encouraging thing is that it's starting to get a lot better. Natwest are pioneering with a scheme for a five-year break, with pension safeguards and guaranteed retraining at the end of it: it will be a long time before that becomes universal, if indeed it ever does, but it's a breakthrough just the same.

The final piece of philosophy concerns the quality of your own work: it's only natural to want to be good at it and get things right, especially with your woman- and Superwoman-taught conditioning. But mistakes do happen, and some tasks do only need to be done adequately. Nobody can be exceptional without let-up; the middle-of-the-road competent is just as necessary as the high-flier all the time, and sometimes gets further in the end; it's always the genius who cracks up. Whether you want to avail yourself of it or not, you have just as much right to be mediocre as everyone else, and as long as you're sure you're doing yourself justice there is nothing you need feel guilty about.

Right, you've turned your mind inside out and discovered you'd be more effective if you only worked one week a year and spent two days of that talking, a third off sick, and half the other two out to lunch. But guess what? – the mountain in your in-tray hasn't suddenly dwindled into a mole-hill, new crises still arrive hot on the heels of the old, and somehow you don't believe thinking differently about things is going to change them much. So now we come to the really hard bit – the practical self-help course.

It's hard, because only you can decide whether to take any advice, and if you're more than halfway trapped you won't believe it's possible. So the first step is to give a copy of this book to a colleague and make sure she reads it, so that when she catches you out she can tease you or bully you into catching yourself next time. (Two of us once lasted a whole day refusing to get involved in somebody else's problems, just by catching each other when either of our nerves looked like breaking and speaking stern words. I regret to say my nerve broke first – at the time I thought it was a signal victory, because she had such a bad case of overconscientiousness: looking back, I'm not so sure . . .) Seriously, it is immensely helpful if you can find someone else in the same position as you, *and who also recognizes she is in it*, with whom you can join forces to bully each other out of your wilder excesses. If she works with you, so much the better; if not, she should be someone who at least understands the mechanics of your business, otherwise you'll get out of it by saying 'Ah, but you see that doesn't work in *our* firm . . .'

You will laugh mirthlessly if I simply tell you to work the hours you are paid for: so would your employer, no doubt. Overwork (your overwork, that is), is an addiction for both of you and not only will you find a hundred and one emergency reasons for maintaining your dosage, and be able to explain lucidly and at length exactly why they are all paramount, but you might even suffer unpleasant side-effects if your employer were faced with cold turkey. So instead of making any sudden, unkeepable resolutions, you must learn to withdraw slowly.

You do this by making unbreakable engagements. Arrange for the gas man to call at 8.30 a.m. (if you can!) one day. Book lunch with a friend and then leave your address book at home so you can't cancel, or make a 1 p.m. hair appointment. Shut the cat out for the day, or agree to let in a neighbour's child at 6.30 p.m. Don't do anything silly, like going mad and trying to do all these things on the same day, or booking a manicure in the middle of the trade fair: choose for each of them a perfectly ordinary day, when nobody could conceivably accuse you of being selfish, thoughtless, or just plain bloody-minded. And notice that I'm deliberately not suggesting anything that involves effort – the advanced stuff comes later! All you have to do is be somewhere, say one day a week, with a commitment as unbreakable as Tupperware. You'll be surprised how easy it is. And I prophesy that when you hear the comments of 'Half day, is it?' you collect, you'll realize just how much of a habit your long hours have become to everyone. You will probably even defend yourself: 'It *is* lunchtime/5.30/only 9.30. you know'. Good. Do it for, say, six weeks running and you'll begin to recognize what are working hours and what aren't. You might even get to enjoy it.

The next step, I'm sorry to say, is Superwoman's old favourite gospel, organization. Shirley Conran coined the maxim 'You have to be efficient if you are going to be lazy', and though I'd substitute 'sane' for 'lazy' I'm afraid it's still absolutely true. But by efficient, I don't mean creating a revolutionary new filing system in your paper-clip box: it's much more a question of using your time properly. Now you've learnt how to recognize 'free' time, you need to recognize working time. In other words, even if you're used to being in the office until seven, that's no excuse for not starting your work until ten – if you started at nine-thirty, you'd be through by six-thirty. I know it sounds like the exact opposite of what I've said so far, but it isn't: just a matter of getting your time-scale back into focus.

You will also find that you can do things faster if you have the necessary information to hand, not buried under six inches of dross. If you aren't yet ready to cope with a regular weekly filing session – and I'm not, so I don't see why you should be – try at least to rummage through your in-tray once a day, chucking the clutter into 'pending', 'filing' or 'bin', and leaving yourself with the slim outline you always wanted. It's astonishing how many letters that seemed on Monday to need replies can on Friday do quite well without, and how much bumf needn't sit there winking beadily at you for a month before you throw it away. It's equally astonishing how quickly the essential paperwork can be dealt with if you just do it, instead of transferring it from tray to tray and list to list until it has assumed the proportions of an EEC directive.

Priorities also need sorting out. When you make your list of 'Things to do today' – and unless you are too far gone in despair, I'm sure you have one – go through it again and number everything in order of importance. It sounds obvious, it only takes two minutes, but it really helps. You never remember them in the right order when you're writing them down, and I've often been paralysed into total inactivity by a list on which number one wasn't needed until March – but number eight was needed last week.

And the most obvious priority of all: your work comes before anyone else's, so you need to start disembarrassing yourself of all that peripheral activity. If you've never learned how to change a typewriter ribbon (my one ace) or to mend the photocopier, you can't reasonably expect yourself to do it, but I suppose you might have gone blindly ahead and learnt before you read this. Well, if you need to type and there's nobody around to sort out the ribbon for you, then it's not normal working hours and you shouldn't be there at all; but if you must, then there must also be another vacant typewriter you can use instead. Supposing the photocopier doesn't respond to fifty minutes of kicks and cajolery? You'll have to wait for the engineer anyway, so you might as well use the fifty minutes for something constructive. Can you live without coffee long enough for someone else's nerve to snap – or are you really buying it to suit yourself, and blaming it on them? And you could delegate Fred's collection to your poor secretary to keep her from screaming with boredom while you're dithering about not having anything else to give her (speaking of which, don't you think she could at least *draft* that report?) Ask expectantly at the beginning of the meeting who is taking the minutes – you must give the rest a chance to play martyr sometimes – or if you do want to take them yourself, again establish the fact first: then you can't feel put-upon.

It's more difficult to avoid helping out when you're asked to. It seems churlish to refuse – and which particular straw deserves the unhappy distinction of being the back-breaker? Besides, you certainly don't want to risk being confused with the 'other woman', the one who gave the sex a bad name and gave you so much reason to fall into the Superwoman Trap in the first place. (You know her: always too busy to do anything that doesn't fall within her extremely limited definition of her job, but somehow with plenty of time for a long and distracting account of last night's episode of *Dallas* at the top of her voice, and very quick to add insult to injury by asking *you* to help *her*.) If it is her asking for help, you may have to fall back on a promise to find some time tomorrow, when you know it'll be too late, and then feel wretched with unreasonable guilt. If it's someone else, then it could be a genuine emergency – in which case you will recognize it, you're far too bossy not to know about all possible crises – or else the supplicant is either a man conditioned to 'ask Nanny' (let him do up his own buttons for once; he'll never learn younger) or a Trap-ee too, and worse off than yourself if she can't *see* how busy you are.

Well, at least you can *tell* yourself that. But you probably *will* help, so just try to do it constructively – suggest a quicker way of doing things, or do a routine task together, or offer the loan of your last document in the same style. But don't just do the job yourself. That way, not only will you be permanently lumbered, but they'll never learn for themselves, and they really *won't* know what's hit them if you suddenly withdraw privileges.

You may be disappointed that I haven't suggested anything dramatic, or even cut-and-dried. But I am assuming that you do care about your job and that overworking is as natural to you as breathing: you wouldn't be in the Superwoman Trap if you didn't, or not this particular form of it, anyway. If you want me to tell you you're hard done by, I will – though I will remind you that, as you've seen, it's as much your own fault as anyone else's – but I won't tell you to sit back and wait for the world to drop a living into your lap. And if you really are in the Superwoman Trap you wouldn't thank me for being unrealistic about your commitments, real and imagined. Until there is real equality in the workplace on both fronts – equal opportunity and reward for women, and equal recognition by women that they're not the only perfect one – then a woman's work will always be fraught with injustices, inconsistencies and frustrations. Still, even if all you have gained from this chapter is an idea that there might be separate hours dividing office and home – read on, and see how much worse it can be when you get there!

# 3
# *Moonlighting*

Unless you *are* Superwoman, you don't come home from work to put the casserole you prepared last night in the oven before running a relaxing bath, changing into something comfortable but slinky, whisking through the kitchen and sitting-room for half an hour to restore the ordered comfort around you, and then settle down for a stimulating evening with your man or half a dozen friends, or a quiet one catching up on your correspondence or working on a chair cover. Nor do you spend your weekends either entertaining friends – a children's party during the day, then a civilized adult dinner – having got up at the crack of dawn on Saturday to get the best of the early produce in the market and turn it into delicious exotica with extra for the freezer; or alternatively scouring antique shops on Saturday, restoring your 'find' on Sunday, and landscaping the garden in between.

On weekdays, you're much more likely to do one of two things:

1. Tear through the door, dropping bulging carrier bags where they fall, feed the cat, attack the kitchen, and whirl round frantically trying to keep abreast of the chores before collapsing in front of the television.

2. Slump in, head straight for the gin bottle, kick the cat, and spend the evening in a catatonic trance in front of the television worrying that you're not keeping abreast with the chores.

You couldn't do it Superwoman's way in any case: you didn't manage to prepare anything last night (in fact, you're not even sure if there is anything to eat); the water is only lukewarm because the boiler is having a fit of temperament; there aren't any clean clothes to change into even if you could be bothered; to create any sort of order in *your* home would take more like a day than half an hour – and who's got the energy for stimulating company or chatty letter-writing after the day you've had? In fact, by the time you've trudged round the late-night supermarket, rescued the milk and bills from the doorstep, realized you've forgotten to buy coffee, washed up enough pans to make supper in, and cooked it, all you're ready for is bed.

And then the weekends are terrible. On Friday night you allow yourself to give in and do nothing with a clear conscience; you've had a tiring week, and anyway you can do it tomorrow, but Saturday and Sunday are distinctly unrelaxing. Saturday morning always seems to disappear completely into the supermarket trolley, and if you're not careful *Grandstand* will catch you unawares when you get back and next thing you know it's five o'clock. If you avoid the sport, you will end up ploughing through the washing and ironing, or hoovering your world to within an inch of its life, or doing something about the garden, or cooking vast quantities of food to put in the freezer for next week, none of which will somehow be exactly right for the occasion when you come to defreeze it . . . Sundays have gone by the time you've read the papers, washed the car and dealt with Sunday lunch, and suddenly it's *Mastermind*, you're absolutely exhausted, and you've only done a quarter of the tasks you had planned. If you try to go away for the weekend, or spend it in half-remembered irresponsible pleasures like window-shopping, or sleeping, or going to the theatre (but when will you find time to organize the tickets?), you can't escape the guilt pangs, and you end up not enjoying yourself at all or at the very least feeling so bad that you might as well not have.

Superwoman has been up to her old tricks again with our career-girl housekeeping, persuading us that we can meld her two working lives into one and become living proof of her rosy ideal of a fulfilled, stimulating business life cushioned by the calm haven of a pleasant, smooth-running home. It has an enormously strong appeal – no wonder we want to make it come true. It may even, from the outside, look as if it *is* true: why shouldn't it, when we are working hard to create just that illusion? Why should our friends ever see – or why would we want them to – what we know only too well; that our haven of peace in an ever-sprinning world is spinning fast as fast as the rest of it? That the ideal and the illusion are both just a cover-up for a precarious state of barely-contained chaos?

However compact and labour-saving your home, however many gadgets you amass, however few encumbrances you have, the most you can do is to gloss over the surface during the week and cope with the most pressing maintenance problems at the weekend, but usually without ever feeling totally in control. A minor problem like a light-bulb dying, or running out of eggs, can endanger your equilibrium, and anything major, such as a malfunctioning boiler or an exploding vacuum cleaner, can bring the whole house of cards down on your head. Your situation will obviously be more or less precarious depending on your individual circumstances and character – just what time you get home from the office, how good you are at remembering what you need to buy, how houseproud you are anyway, but most of all who you share your home with; whether it's just you and the goldfish, or flatmates, or a live-in man, or a full-blown family. But whichever particular circumstances apply to you, it will probably still go very much against the grain to believe for a moment that you, who are so professional, so talented, so hardworking, can possibly be capable of less than perfection in a simple task like running a household.

The more thoroughly committed you are to the Superwoman Trap at work, the more trapped you also become at home, and vice versa. There is a kind of puritanism in the Superwoman myth that always manages to make one feel one should be working hardest at what one likes least. So if you're in the office ten hours a day, you tell yourself you're in danger of becoming a workaholic and neglecting your own life, so you owe it to yourself to spend more time *on* yourself – in other words, being a house/parlourmaid. If you secretly yearn for more time at home and nourish an arcane fetish for defrosting the fridge or polishing brass, you tell yourself you must forget these old-fashioned recidivist leanings towards domesticity and concentrate on fulfilling your true potential as an equal contender in the Rat Race. If you have a live-in man, you may talk tough about equal housework but you will also secretly worry that he'll leave you if you feed him take-away Chinese and surly answers too often; if you have children, that they will grow up inarticulate and maladjusted for lack of attention; if you live alone, that you will become isolated and end up living like Quentin Crisp amid aeons of dust and dereliction. The less you really care about the maternal/domestic role, the more you will convince yourself of these dangers, so that guilt makes you more obsessive about it than if you secretly really liked it in the first place. And since I can't believe anyone *really* likes washing up, that tends to be hard on the career-orientated Trap-ee.

The fact is that nobody can do two jobs at once; if you want a perfect home as well as a career – as opposed to a job – you will have to pay somebody to help you create it, and if you can't or don't want to do that, then you'll have to settle for less than perfection. There is a happy medium between a constant diet of Coronation Street and one of Coronation Chicken, and whether you are currently paralysed into the one or galvanized into the other, or both alternately, it is possible to find it.

The would-be Superwoman often tends to dismiss out of hand the possibility of employing help, partly because we refuse to believe it should be necessary if we were properly organized, partly because we are no longer comfortable, as a society, with the idea of servants, and partly because we think we can't afford it. But you should think carefully before you convince yourself of the validity of any of these lines of reasoning. There is no God-given rule that thou shalt do everything thyself, even if you could: Superwoman's genius is based very largely on her organizational abilities, rather than her specific talents. Today's domestic workers are a long way from the music-hall caricature image of Mrs Mopp – one of the results of equal opportunities is that their job is a job to them, just as yours is to you, not the demeaning necessity it once was – and nannies and childminders are no Sarey Gamps. As for the financial cost: we tend to think we can't afford domestic help because we think in terms of its prewar levels, and the only establishments where even an approximation of those levels exist today are those of the very, very rich. But the cost of a pair of theatre tickets can pay for a morning's domestic help a week, which will make a considerable difference. If you have two incomes and a family which needs enough domestic help to eat up rather more money than that, you may consider, before you decide it is uneconomic and you should give up work instead and be better off, whether your job is important primarily for its financial benefits, or whether it is more important to you than that. It's no good being financially better off and miserable in a gleaming home if what you really enjoy and are good at is the intricacies of your import/export business.

If you do have help, you *must* resist the temptation to clear up before it: how would you feel if you arrived in the office every day to find that somebody from another department had started all your work for you? I know it is a natural reaction to make some attempt at tidying up before inviting anyone into your home, but in this case it does rather defeat the object of the invitation, as well as being insulting to the employee. You should also sort out clearly at the very beginning exactly what types of work you want done and what not done: there is no point paying someone to polish the doorknobs when what you really want is the laundry out of the way, or vice versa. Every domestic cleaner has their own rules, as well, about what they will and will not do – you simply have to make sure that they fit in with your requirements before you get stuck with them, or you risk being as badly off timewise and worse off financially than you were in the first place.

Whether or not you employ help in the home, you need to work out which particular tasks are essentials, which priorities, and which real bugbears. These will not be the same as the ones laid out in Mrs Beeton or even *Superwoman*, and won't even necessarily be the ones instilled in you at your mother's knee. By essentials I mean genuine necessities, like changing nappies, or feeding yourself plus any other members of the household incapable of doing the same, or washing a shirt for the morning, not frivolities like dusting, or cleaning windows, or washing up after every meal. They are things that will have to be tackled daily, and simply can't be got out of except by being delegated to somebody else, but there are encouragingly few of them. You will also have to allow time during the week for your priorities; the things that matter to you personally, not to Mrs Beeton. If you can leave the house happily unhoovered for a month but detest a toothpaste-spattered washbasin, if you don't mind a week's worth of washing-up piled in the sink but cringe at an unpolished light switch then, within certain basic limits of hygiene, just follow your inclinations and blow your training in good housekeeping at least until Saturday. A list of these, numbered in order of importance, probably won't stretch to more than half-a-dozen really top-level fetishes: combine this list with your rock-bottom essentials, and experiment with ignoring absolutely everything else on weekdays except in dire emergencies, such as mothers-in-law descending. You'll be astonished how well you can survive.

What chores loom large in your nightmares, and why? Do you really loathe ironing, or do you just loathe the *idea* of it so much that it has now built up into a monument of terror in the airing cupboard and you couldn't face it because of its sheer magnitude? Do you hate washing up, or do you hate doing it in lukewarm greasy water? Would a new vacuum improve your relationship with your carpets, or is your dislike more ingrained than the crumbs?

If you look at your bugbears in this way you will find that in some cases you don't actually dislike the chore any more than you actively dislike cleaning your teeth – you would just rather put it off if you could, and of course any mildly unpleasant experience, once put off for long enough, becomes a true horror. On the other hand, you will also be able to identify those chores you really do hate, or the factors in them that make them hateful, and either delegate them, or adapt them. (I used to think, for example, that I hated ironing; when I worked out that what I really hated was folding ironed shirts I started keeping them on hangers instead, and life improved dramatically.) Some, of course, will simply be unavoidable nastinesses, but then so is travelling to work in the rush hour or checking the accounts, and you probably don't even think about the possibility of avoiding either of them.

Quite apart from the normal tedious housebound round of chores, there are certain time-sensitive problem areas which are problems only for somebody who works out of the home. The one I always find particularly difficult during the week is shopping. Not everyone works within easy carrying distance of a full range of shops, or indeed can always be sure of having time to visit them in a lunch hour, and even if you do, and can, then unless you drive to the office you can face an arm-breaking trip home as you try to juggle with the potatoes and the strap-hanging at the same time. But supermarkets have – either fortunately or unfortunately depending on how you look at it –, got wise to the fact that many women now work during the day, so they stay open near your home until eight, and then you feel morally bound to call in on your way back. If you get back too late for even these extended hours, you feel both guilty and put-upon for being so ruled by your working life; if you can manage to get there, you do, which not only always seems to work out expensive, but means you have no excuse for not cooking a proper meal instead of the frozen pizza the old corner shop would have provided. And the most irritating thing of all is that even if you end up shopping every evening, the Saturday morning trip is mysteriously always still necessary, and *always* still costs the same amount, while if you try to be efficient and buy a week's supplies on Saturday there is still never anything left to eat by Tuesday: this phenomenon never ceases to astonish me. On the other hand, an equally amazing discovery is that if you don't buy anything at all for a week, you don't starve.

Even if you can get somebody to undertake the physical activity of shopping for you, there is still The List. Your partner, in particular, is unlikely to be satisfied with being told to buy 'something for supper' – he wants to know what. Even if you can dredge up some idea of what people eat over the phone in the middle of an office crisis or on the station platform, you've got to tell them exact quantities, and brand names where relevant, and quite often give them a verbal map of the shop as well, and then they'll come back with the wrong sort of beans and no butter: it is at times like these that the idea of a permanent diet of alternating fish fingers and hamburgers or dinner out can become very seductive.

If you have managed to get the commissariat organized, there is always the specialist problem of livestock. Children and animals cannot be ignored, and both fall into the category of woman's work. They need feeding, cleaning, walks and attention; they are subject to alarming illnesses and strange behavioural patterns which need at best worrying about and at worst time-consuming remedies; they need minders when you can't be there, with all the organization that involves; they are never conducive to a relaxed routine. Animals are obviously altogether easier to deal with, but both need a reasonably regular timetable, which can play havoc with the promotional prospects of being available to snatch opportunities as they come up as well as with your humbler hopes of an ordered home life.

Electricity and gas appliances, television and telephones, need regular servicing and occasional emergency attention; doctors and vets work the same sort of hours you do; burst pipes do not wait until you have time to deal with them. And even if you have a partner whom you could reasonably expect to share, not just the telephoning, but the staying in or coming home early that these and other emergencies will entail, it is surprising how vital even the most liberated man's 10 a.m. appointment can become when it comes to the crunch.

Of course, if you have domestic help a lot of these time-sensitive problems can be arranged in such a way that they can be dealt with without either of you having to be present; even if you haven't, neighbours are normally a tremendous help as stand-bys. And the ones that do require one of you will have to be dealt with on an *ad hoc* bargaining basis – if I arrange for the gas man to come when you can be there, I'll do it next time, or I'll stay in with the sick child if you'll do the shopping and phone for the prescription. You'll probably find that it never quite works out equitably, but even a minor victory like the concession that your conference is more important than his lunch is a step in the right direction.

Housework as such will be dealt with more thoroughly in the next chapter: for the moonlighter what is important is to learn to juggle her two roles with some semblance of success, and particularly vital is to keep sight of your own desires and inclinations. You are paid to work at your salaried job, so there is every justification for taking it seriously and even, given the universal pressures of career-ism, sometimes taking it too seriously. But everything outside the office door is supposed to be *your* life, run *your* way and primarily for *your* benefit – not an endless battle to keep under control an existence that often seems determined to prove the possibility of perpetual motion.

What are you running a home *for*, if not for you to live in? Yet all too frequently you seem to be coming home from one job only to start on another, and the whole concept of a personal life gets ground out altogether between their twin mill-stones. Superwoman may have one dimension for her career, a separate, parallel one for her household duties, a third, different from either, for running a job and a home, and another for her hobbies and social life, but the most you can cram into your human pint pot is at least some element of each – and the fourth one is by no manner of means the least essential. So getting out and doing things should be your reason for getting out *of* doing things: that's what you need the time for, not for fitting in more and more chores.

And at least if you swallow your guilt pangs and sail out to dinner one night, that's one fewer day's worth of shopping, cooking and washing-up to worry about; given the strange paradox of supermarket shopping, it won't make a significant difference if you spend the weekend in Sussex instead of Sainsbury's; it is also just conceivable that the sky won't fall in if you write a ten-page letter to your best friend instead of pressing your best dress. This applies to time off work as well: half an hour missed one morning may not be worth as much as the fact you've done the washing-up while waiting for the telephone to be mended.

Those things that do need some attention during the week are best done immediately you get in. They *are* work, after all, so treat them as an extension of the working day, preferably with the promise of a treat when you've finished them. If you prepare supper and put the towels in the washing machine in the same mental breath as taking off your coat, then it only takes as long as the time actually used – say forty minutes – and you can sit down to a drink in front of the latest mini-series with the virtuous feeling of something achieved. But if you sit down first you won't get up again for at least an hour, and half your mind will be on the gloomy prospect of chores yet to do with no treat in store because you're already having that – so it will feel as if it's already taken you half the evening before you've done anything constructive at all. And those things you've decided to relegate to the weekends, for heaven's sake *do* relegate: if you're going to sit biting your nails about the onion skins on the kitchen floor you might as well sweep them up here and now and have done, rather than making yourself neurotic about them. And there is no point in making work for yourself unnecessarily: you may think he'll leave you if you don't cook him Boeuf en Croute, but he'd be just as happy with grilled chops and a lot happier without the moans about how long it's taken to do. Besides, why isn't *he* cooking tempting delicacies for you?

Many moonlighting would-be Superwomen do find it easier to convince themselves of the need to give time to themselves during the week, because the career angle of the trap encourages them to see the importance of being relaxed for the new day's work if not for their own well-being, than at weekends. There is then a double danger of falling into paralysis in the evenings, and treating the weekend as a repository for every tedious task under the sun, from painting your nails to painting the ceiling. As far as the evening paralysis is concerned, I find that I actually feel less exhausted the more I do (though I can work quite hard at telling myself this is a lie), probably because a sense of achievement is more relaxing than the pressured expectation of hard work still to come.

The two major mistakes with weekends are firstly, treating them as one continuous block of time, and secondly trying to fit major achievements as well as a full week's quota of routine maintenance into them. A corollary of this second error occurs when you have a partner and you both reach the weekend with firm but different ideas of your aims for it – he's decided to spring-clean the sitting-room, say, while you're determined that this is the week you're going to find the right shade of paint for the bathroom. This is disconcerting and in severe cases disorientating, like when you're told on Saturday morning you're driving half across the country for a specialist car- part, while you thought you were going to stock up the freezer (it happened!), but it can and should be avoided by spending some of the new free time in the evenings talking to each other. The two main errors need more radical readjustment.

The weekend consists of two days and one evening, and each day can be divided into three sections of morning, afternoon and evening. Friday evening can be largely discounted from the home-work point of view; you will want to use it to relax in, secure in the knowledge of a week well over and two days' grace before the next one begins. But for the rest of the time, it is a dangerous principle to decide 'I'll do that this weekend': you will probably either try to do it all on Saturday morning or end up leaving everything until Sunday afternoon. You should think about confining achievements to one or two sections with well-spaced treats in the intervening ones, unless your aim for this particular weekend is a radical one like staying with those friends you haven't seen since they moved to Dorset, or rebuilding the garden shed, in which case all regular life will have to stop for the duration, and you can cope with the guilt and the lack of clean shirts as best you may. So you could do the shopping and clean out the store cupboard on Saturday morning, say, then have a pub lunch, write letters and pay bills in the afternoon, clean one room in the evening, and spend Sunday cooking or laundering before going out to dinner or a film.

You should limit your aims for the weekend to one major or a handful of minor ones each time. So if you decide you're going to paint the hall, you should concentrate on just that, and full-scale meals will be out of the reckoning; if you're planning to catch up on a week's cleaning and two weeks' laundry, don't imagine you'll plant out the flower bed as well; a quest for the perfect wallpaper doesn't mix well with a full day's cooking programme. If you set yourself either too many targets or no targets at all, you will inevitably tire yourself out flitting from one thing to another, probably finishing none of them and certainly feeling that you haven't achieved enough, if anything, by bedtime on Sunday. An attainable goal, on the other hand, can always be reached, and you may even give yourself a wonderful glow of success by outstripping it: you will then come to Sunday evening feeling confident and refreshed.

There is no denying that the general business of living can be pretty hard on moonlighters, but you do have one distinct advantage over your housebound counterparts. You can set your career and your home pressures against each other as counter-irritants. A delicious sorbet does wonders for an ego bruised by an inconclusive day's bargaining, and the knowledge of a deal well-struck for the inadequacies of the dusting. If life is tough on the parallel bars, it's got a lot more scope than on the single beam . . .

# 4

# *Only a Housewife*

Superwoman is *never* 'only a housewife'; she is a fulfilled and caring wife and mother (usually) or home manager (occasionally) with her own outside interests. Although by the very nature of the beast she *has* worked for a salary, she has adapted smoothly and gracefully to working for the housekeeping money instead – in fact, she throws herself into the job of running a home with all the professionalism of a modern Mrs Beeton. Every day, she provides two well-balanced cooked meals (breakfast and supper – lunch too, if she has children at home) off matching modern china at the round pine table, making extra for the freezer at the same time, and she knocks up a batch of jam or a couple of 'cut and come again' cakes once a week. She buys basics in bulk from the local cash-and-carry or hypermarket, and neither she nor her well-stocked cupboard will blench at dinner for the boss at two hours' notice. Her cleaning routine covers the whole house within a week, including doing the windows and defrosting the fridge as well as her daily checklist of laundry, bed-making, washing up and vacuuming. She likes gardening so much that she isn't content with her sculptured half-acre and the herb garden on the kitchen windowsill, but also tends a positive jungle in assorted jardinieres around the house (even those evil-looking large things with bits out of their leaves which look horrible unless they're brushed with milk every hour or so: hers look marvellous). She decorates the house herself, with lots of white, pastels, dramatic deep green or French blue and Laura Ashley in the living areas, bright primary colours in the nursery, mirrors in the bathroom, clinical white or natural pine in the kitchen and the child's own choice however ghastly, in teenage bedsits – it's their room, it's important that they shouldn't feel outside influences there. She may even mix her own paints, and achieve unusual effects with dragging, or toning shades, or texturing: she certainly makes the curtains and matching cushions, and grudges no time or money spent on finding exactly the right colour paint or style of wallpaper to set off Aunt Ethel's marquetry cabinet to the best advantage. She copes efficiently with the basic electrical and carpentry jobs around the house, does her own upholstery and sews and knits stylishly and, if she does need outside help with anything, has a whole collection of 'little' men and women to call on. The labrador is well-trained, well-groomed and well-exercised, and never goes upstairs. She is always careful to remember, however, that her husband is the most important person in her life, and the evenings are set aside for his comfort and beguilement at home, or on a sortie to the theatre or to dinner at least once a week. All this, however, is not enough to keep her occupied, so she almost always has some sideline to stop her from vegetating, ranging from a mere evening class when the baby is very young, through part-time work at home to keep her hand in, to a three-day-a-week antique business when the system can run itself with less supervision. She is very modest about her organization, and gives the credit to her labour-saving devices, her treasure of a home-help, or the wonderful support she gets from her family.

She is also, of course, a fantastic mother, but that is a topic that deserves a chapter all of its own.

Superwoman is either going back to work as soon as the children are old enough, or she is staying within the home through choice. For the rest of the world it isn't necessarily that easy. A friend who was an assistant matron had to move when her GP husband found a job in another part of the country: by moving to a different health district before finding a new job she automatically demoted herself to staff nurse – a job she can't handle while she has preschool children. Another went on maternity leave and while she was away the firm went bust. A senior advertising executive and a highly-qualified accountant both had to choose between their demanding jobs and seeing their children occasionally. A high-powered scientific publisher married a man who was promptly sent to the Far East – there isn't a lot of scope for her talents and experience in Malaysia. Others feel that they must devote their time to motherhood for as long as it takes, or follow their men around the country every couple of years, sacrificing their career to his, or look after ailing parents. They all made ccertain choices, but not to become housewives.

These homebound would-be Superwomen tend to fall into four different categories. There is the second-class citizen: 'I'm afraid I'm just a housewife; boring, isn't it?', accompanied by self-deprecating giggles. Or the human dynamo: 'Sit down and have a cup of coffee – Oh, no, sorry, not there, that's the ironing . . . do you mind tea, I can't find the instant? Oh yes, I should have warned you, that paint's wet', accompanied by gestures too varied and exhausting to describe. Or the would-have-been Superwoman: 'Of course, I'd have been a partner by now if it hadn't been for Ian's job/Miranda coming along/mother's sciatica', accompanied by jabbing finger in the general direction of the offending party. Or the tub-thumping apostle: 'It's so rewarding . . . I don't understand how any woman can bear to miss out on her child growing up/work when there aren't enough jobs for men', accompanied by a determined lack of interest in the latest film, and a tendency to interrupt with the information that the gas man came today.

What the four have in common is discontent and a whacking great inferiority complex. The first two want to do the job perfectly, like Superwoman does; the last two don't want to do it at all; and the first, at least, also wants it to be recognized as worthwhile. But whichever category you come into, and I'm sure you'll deny them all, there are two distinct problems facing you – the work itself, and its status. And since status is likely to be the deeper-seated of the two, let's look at it first.

There has been a fair amount of controversy in the press lately about job snobbery, and the fact that it is spreading to women – in other words, where only men used automatically to dismiss the little woman as a sub-species, career women are now joining in. Just because your gossip is about the burst boiler and the new couple at number 28 instead of about the day the lift broke down between floors and Mr Wilson in accounts, it's supposed for some reason to be less interesting, and somehow invalidates your opinion on the invasion of Tasmania as well. And it does seem very hard that your traditional allies, your sisters, should be turning on you too. I imagine that most working women would have to admit to having caught themselves asking 'And what do you do?' at a drinks party, and to being momentarily silenced by the answer 'I'm a housewife' – usually because there isn't a stock response to it in our party-going vocabulary. You can't say a polite 'How interesting' without being incredibly patronizing; you can't ask 'What does that involve, exactly?' because you know, or you ought to; you can't solicit an opinion on the question of a 'housewife's wage' without breaking all the party-going rules by getting too serious. But even if the question 'What do you do?' has become just another formula like '*How* do you do?', it's a formula based on the assumption of a certain range of available answers, and to assume that every woman under forty has a career is just as untenable as the old assumption that none did. But to be fair, a lot of this job snobbery is inverted: the housewife, if she's of the Superwoman generation, is used to salaried work, and is quite as guilty as those still doing it of believing that it carries extra status. Her normal reaction, therefore, tends to be either an embarrassing self-apology or a boring self-justification.

Since I haven't yet been 'only a housewife', I asked a number of friends how they felt about this status gap, and got some pretty unsatisfactory replies. Either they pointed out hotly that they were going back to work in a couple of months anyway, or that they were working from home or part-time, and thus had simply adapted their careers rather than dropping them, or they didn't know what I was talking about, they worked a darn sight harder than they ever had before, and in any case it was all so wonderfully enriching and I should try it some time. Only one, serenely happy and confident in her chosen mix of freelancing and home-making, said that yes, she had noticed these attitudes among her friends but it had simply never occurred to her to feel inadequate – just lucky.

And yet the status of domestic work has historically always been high. A housekeeper was, up to the Second World War, someone of considerable importance: of such importance, in fact, that in the largest establishments the control of the household was normally held by a man. The Comptroller of the Royal Household was in Europe a position carrying a good deal of political kudos, and similar titles gave their Eastern holders virtual autonomy. In a large, though not even noble, British household the housekeeper could control up to fifty people, while even in the most straitened she would preside over a couple of girls and maybe an 'outside man'. Lower down the servant hierarchy the status was still firmly in favour of the domestic staff, united in their contempt of the – male – under-gardeners and stable lads, and a woman would consider herself much more fortunate to land a job as a parlourmaid than to take work in the local mill. And nowadays a new generation of domestic workers, who are almost as likely to be male as female, are sensibly claiming back that prestige for their profession, and soon it will only be the Superwoman generation who are stuck with their erroneous view of housework as a low-status occupation.

What happened was the Second World War, which left the middle classes high and dry. Brought up to expect at least one live-in-maid, they found themselves with a daily help if they were lucky; families were smaller, too, and the greater possibility of doing without help contributed to its greater morality: by the sixties there had been a further shift, with egalitarianism spreading like wildfire, and the subsequent arrival of the socially ambivalent *au pair*, who could cause a crisis of etiquette by being better 'born' than her employers. Clearly, some readjustment was needed. It would be impossible, immoral classism to feel demeaned by the lack of housemaids: therefore the sense of lost caste was transferred to the work itself. And since this fitted in very well with the growth of the Women's Rights movement and its claims for the mental upgrading of women, housework per se was downgraded to become yet another of the chains binding womankind to her slavery. And this merging of a mere thirty years of changing social beliefs has come to represent our traditional role – poor old housework!

So since housework itself isn't demeaning, maybe it's the lack of subordinates that is? Well, if you do a quick review of your salaried acquaintances and the number of junior staff under their control, you'll probably find that one or two is a reasonable quota, half a dozen good going, and the majority of friends of your own age will be like ministers without portfolio – managers without anyone to manage. So you may only have a home-help to direct, or you may be, like them, a housekeeper without housemaids: what's the difference?

There is, of course, one radical difference. You have almost certainly forfeited your financial independence, and there is no point in pretending that doesn't matter because it does. Contrary to the cartoon image, in which women rush out to buy fur coats on his account the minute he's caught the 8.15, most of us loathe the thought of being even partially dependent on somebody else's money. It's all right when you both earn different amounts: you both contribute to the kitty but what's over is your own. It's even just about bearable to spend someone else's money on household expenses, though it raises all sorts of moral questions when you disagree about the colour of the curtains for the bathroom. But for one's own little private luxuries, it can be intolerable. Most women I know who *do* earn, including me, religiously pay back – oh, in irregular instalments and without interest, but pay back – the cost of holidays and dinners they can't afford and wouldn't ever have bought left to themselves, to men who earn in many cases twice what they do: how much worse, then, to feel guilty about every pair of tights or bar of chocolate you buy!

It is trite but true to say that money isn't everything. It is just one of the many and varied contributions necessary to running a home, or a business, or indeed to do anything at all, and it's just bad luck that it's easily the most tangible and marketable. But you wouldn't expect to put a financial stake into the company that pays you a wage – your contribution there is your expertise and eight hours' labour a day. The same holds good for the household. You must have seen at least one of those periodic surveys that turn up in the papers on what 'only a housewife' should cost at the going market rate, but you may not have seen the point. They do tend to dwell unrealistically on the remote prospect of a government-paid housewife's wage, rather than on the much more important principle behind that dream – the point is that you are paying, through service, just as much into the household as the person who contributes money. You are thereby freeing that money for commodities that would not otherwise be affordable, as well as for those which unimaginatively demand payment in currency, and at the same time you are freeing the wage-earner from a considerable amount of drudgery. The labourer is worthy of her hire, and that means you can stop feeling guilty about your new pair of shoes or the not-strictly-necessary food processor: the latter is a tool of your trade, and you have fairly earned the former, and much more besides, through your labours as domestic, laundress, cook, childminder, decorator and all those other multifarious skills you need to be 'only a housewife'.

So what if you've convinced yourself that the children

are intellectually stimulating and that domestic toil is somehow more valid, more moral, than wage-slavery, and have flicked through the last couple of pages certain that thank heavens, they don't apply to you? You might do well to digest them just the same, in case you're doing a very good cover-up on your inferiority complex. But if you're absolutely sure that you've still chosen the better part, you might remind yourself that Martha was sure of it too when she asked Jesus to make Mary give her a hand, and got sent to the rightabout. Of course children *can* be intellectually stimulating, but they're much more frequently mentally exhausting. The fact that domestic work is just as valid as welding can't ever make it more so; nor can the role of childrearer be *more* creative than the role of teacher, for example. Everyone puts their own skills and inclinations to use as best they can given the limitations of their circumstances, and just as nobody else's choice can invalidate yours, so yours can't invalidate theirs either – it cuts both ways.

And as for that occasional suggestion that 'women shouldn't put men out of a job' (yes, I've heard it used, and recently): well, I suspect that even if you've been stung into using it yourself you know at heart it's utter nonsense. There might conceivably be, one day, if unemployment continues to rise, some justification for restricting wage earning to one person per household, though even if it ever happened the case would be very weak; but there's certainly no reason to assume that the wage-earner should be the man. Maybe the woman could earn more – it happens, though still not often enough – or there could be a host of other reasons for her work taking priority. And until that happens, in any case, you still have no right to condemn your salaried friend for taking a different path from yours. Her financial circumstances may not be as comfortable; she might be the only qualified astrophysicist in Ayrshire; she might simply be better and happier at her job than she would be at yours. Whatever her reasons, she's as entitled to freedom of choice as you are, and even if you feel your freedom has been curtailed through circumstances outside your control it won't help either of you to chip away at hers.

So now you're neither ashamed nor smug about being a housewife any more, but you still think you're not doing it properly, or don't want to be doing it at all. In both cases the answer is the same, and I'm afraid it's back to the good old Superwoman maxims of doing less of it and organizing it better.

I wouldn't presume to follow Shirley Conran in her practical prescriptions: everyone has totally different ideas of how to go about things, and no new list of rules is going to improve on hers. Besides, I launched myself enthusiastically into her catalogue of the minimum you can get away with, and gave up almost immediately in flat despair. It was about four times *more* than I had been getting away with, and as a result I drove myself demented trying to build *up* to that level of work, when the whole idea was that I should be relaxing *down* to it. And by the time I'd plumbed the depths of the shopping checklist and the kitchen filing-cabinet, I felt about as productive as a rather lethargic worm. Here again it is Superwoman's nasty habit of treating your household as a blank canvas on which to paint her ideal picture that defeats her struggling followers: life isn't like that.

For a start, nobody actually designs their home to be as clinically hygenic and efficiently streamlined as a space laboratory, and pretty cheerless it would be if you did. Most homes aren't designed at all, but just grow out of cast-off furniture and bits of sale-bargain carpets, with sudden injections of impractical acquisitions from kind friends or the antique market down the road. Clothes are bought for their looks, not their washing instructions; the bank balance never runs to the more expensive but easier to run washing machine; one doesn't decide against children on the basis of a time and motion study. That goatskin rug may pick up every speck of dirt and shed its hairs everywhere, but it looks and feels gorgeous; you can't afford to change Granny's old saucepans for non-stick, and anyway they have wonderful heavy bases; the Victorian linen press may not be the most practical china cupboard in the world, but that's no reason cold-bloodedly to replace it with chipboard and melamine; and why *should* you have the dog put down to avoid a few muddy pawprints and clawed chair-legs? Superwoman is on a losing wicket trying to persuade you you're going to achieve an ideal home – not with a dog, that furniture, and your fondness for heavy cotton shirts that take a day to iron you're not.

So forget about the checklist of chores that don't apply to you, and consider the logic behind them, that does. Some housework has to be done for all sorts of sensible reasons, like having clean clothes to wear, or food to eat, or avoiding infestations of mice and other nasty health hazards, but quite a lot of it is done with the sole aim of making the place look nice, which may be a laudable aim in its own way, but shouldn't become a fetish. Who do you want it to look nice *for*? If it's for yourself, that's fine, and I agree it would be a pity to hang those beautiful and expensive new curtains round a filthy window which ruins their effect. But if you're mostly concerned with what your mother-in-law or the neighbours will think, or you've just been brought up to regard an immaculate home as an end in itself without ever wondering why, you might stop and ask yourself how much you actually care. It could be difficult to convince anyone, including yourself, that you really *want* half an inch of dust on top of the bookcase, but if you do then it's nobody's business but your own. (Except the person who is presumably paying the bills to keep you at home, in which case give him a duster.) If reading *Middlemarch* will do more for your quality of life than cleaning picture frames, then who's to say you ought to be cleaning the picture frames, and will you really worry terribly if your sheets are blue-white instead of whiter-than-white, or vice versa? Quentin Crisp even went so far as to claim that when dust reaches a certain point it doesn't get any worse, but that was after *years*, and there are limits.

These are obviously extreme and not very serious examples, and you will still feel sluttish if you ask anyone into a messy house, but there are levels of tidiness that are not only unnecessary but actually intimidating to visitors. And even if you do care about the way your home looks for its own sake and yours, you are unlikely to reach ideal home standards because you won't be as organized and labour-saving as the mythical paragon you're trying to emulate. But on the plus side, there will almost certainly be some aspects of housework you actually enjoy. The presupposition behind a lot of Superwoman's time and motion lark is that she hates all chores, and so needs to attack them briskly before she can stop herself, like swallowing cough medicine, but it all falls down if you're lucky enough to *like* ironing, or washing paintwork. (My favourite is defrosting the fridge with a hairdryer, which I only get to do because I'm not organized enough to let it defrost automatically at regular intervals, but only tackle it when I can't shut the door on the ice: that's one of the compensations of not being Superwoman.) You also won't *want* to be ruled entirely by time-saving principles. If you happen to prefer sleeping in sheets and blankets, you will continue to spend longer making beds than if you got a duvet; and just as you haven't callously ditched the dog, so you're not going to start blowing your nose into crumpled handkerchiefs on the sole grounds that not ironing them would save you half an hour a week. You'll continue to end up with take-away hamburgers for supper one day because you felt like spending four hours clearing out the glory-hole, and the next the sitting room will go unvacuumed because you wanted to take all day over an elaborate koulibiac de saumon (which nobody will appreciate) or planting the spring bulbs for the dog to dig up again. Crises, such as the hot water system giving up, will carry on taking you by surprise and upsetting the whole household for at least a day, so you find yourself doing the vital washing for tomorrow at midnight, or eating baked beans because you're using the stove to boil water for a bath.

Superwoman, of course, would adapt her routine to take crises in her stride, and would set aside one afternoon a week for major projects like glory-holes – but think of the element of surprise she's losing! The random approach, with spasmodic binges on housework and long periods doing something interesting instead, has more to recommend it: that way you can genuinely enjoy the feeling of unaccustomed virtue even doing the chores you hate, and you can keep an aura of mystery for your man – about where his socks are, for instance, or how to find the Marmite in your new kitchen filing system. Besides, with a few exceptions, you have to do less housework if you do it less often. Admittedly saucepans, even non-stick ones, don't benefit from three day's hardening, but a floor only takes a seventh as long to vacuum if you do it once a week instead of once a day. And although the most apparently basic things sometimes don't get done, the most extraordinary ones *do*; while however little attention a house has had, it's an odd fact that an hour's determined assault can always make it presentable for any but the most exacting visitor, which must prove something.

Seriously, if you want to achieve sub-Superwoman standards of homecare you can't really do better than set yourself a basic, Superwoman-style routine and stick to it, but applying your own minimum standards rather than hers, and making sure you've provided for plenty of little treats to spur you on. You will have your own prejudices for and against short-cuts, and your own priorities (however much I loathe ironing, for example, I loathe unironed shirts more, and tidy cupboards are more important to me than a tidy sitting room), so incorporate them into your master plan. You will also find life easier if you adopt a routine that suits the way you work – it's no good following the 'Don't put it down, put it away' principle, for instance, if it means you're going to take your gloves into the bedroom, where you find a water glass to go to the kitchen, whither the soap has strayed from the bathroom, where Johnny's dressing gown is adorning the floor: all when you started off with five minutes to clear and set the table. Equally, there's no point in dumping it all in the spare room if you know you'll completely forget about the horrors lurking behind its closed doors until half an hour before Uncle Peter arrives. It is usually better for most people to do one thing and *finish* it, which rules out the spare room trick, because that's not finished, it's left over for the next time. And those tedious chores which simply have to be done are best done first, leaving you with some gloriously esoteric thrill like starching the table linen or grubbing out the drains as a reward afterwards.

Do, also, simplify your life wherever possible by throwing things away. I don't mean the dog, or the pretty rosewood table that wobbles slightly and marks so badly if you put a glass on it, or even your collection of china elephants which are such hell to dust. I mean all those wodges of free magazines and 2p-off toothpaste coupons which sit on the hall table for months; the year-old newspaper you kept for that article on pig-sticking which you know perfectly well you will never now read; the toaster you were going to get a new element for, but haven't; the four sweaters you never wear, and whose absence would take five minutes off the time it takes to shut the drawer; the cardboard box which is such a useful shape, but is always mysteriously just the wrong size for anything – useless clutter, in fact, rather than *objets trouvés*. It only takes a second to sweep the step if you don't have to extricate the broom from a tangle of useful bits of wire and old plant pots; if you do, it becomes a monumental task that you'll waste hours putting off.

And speaking of pot plants, indoor plants are definitely not labour-saving: they seem to need just as much attention as animals and nearly as much as children, but are far likelier than either to repay your efforts by turning brown and shrivelling up. If you like them, then go ahead and have a jungle – but is one sad poinsettia doing a lot for either your decor or your maternal instinct? Pot plants seem to be one of the things Superwoman is supposed to love and be good at, yet it's astonishing how many people, when you say you hate them, come rushing out of their closets to agree with you. The answer seems to be to go in for extremes; if they suit you, have a superabundance, and ignore them totally if they don't – it's the half-hearted compromise that doesn't really work. And unless you're particularly warped, steer clear of cacti: I've been a reluctant landlady to them for years, and you wouldn't believe the places their spines get into . . .

You may, of course, have quite enough gardening to do outside without bringing it indoors as well: the plot does tend to come with the home. Gardens are what might best be called a mixed blessing. After all, it's lovely to have your own luxuriant green sun-trap, bordered by mellow brick walls and a careful disarray of foliage screening the dustbins, the kitchen garden and the children's play area from view of your rockery and velvet lawn. It is less lovely to be responsible for a gone-to-seed wilderness in which bald, football-scarred grass competes with straggling weeds, and the vegetables may be organically insecticide-free but the insects and marauding sparrows have found that out too. Some people like gardening and others don't, as with pot plants, but nobody would call it exactly a restful occupation. If you are the new Percy Thrower then you won't want any advice anyway. If you hate it, then rather than worrying irritably that you aren't doing it you could always turn it into a natural conservation area (until your green-fingered neighbours complain); or pave the whole lot over and restrict the earth – which is at the bottom of the trouble – to a couple of ornamental tubs of bays, magnolias and herbs; or you could stick to flowering shrubs, which don't leave a blank patch when their flowering season is over, and wild strawberries, which are rampant enough ground cover to keep most weeds at bay, and grass, mown just often enough to show willing; or you could get a gardener; or basely divide it up so each child has their own plot to tend (and you get the patio); or, best of all, move into one of those expensive estates set in rolling parkland, where you pay an astronomical fee to have the matter taken out of your hands completely. It might cut down on the privacy of your sunbathing, but it'll leave you a lot more time for it.

Of course, as a would-be Superwoman you won't be satisfied with merely servicing the house and garden: you'll have to decorate as well. Almost every glossy magazine shows you some example of 'an awkward attic' or 'rooms that grow up as they do' or 'dark sophistication for candlelit dinners' at least once a month, and although they nearly never show you how to put up wallpaper or paint the cornice you know that's only because it's so easy you should know already. So naturally all would-be Superwomen have to be interior designers with flair as well as carpenter/handywomen with finesse, and you're probably no exception.

But what if your idea of a well-shaped room is four walls making a square, or your notion of a colour scheme goes no further than white with everything? What if everything looks gorgeous except that there are lumps in the wallpaper, or the colour you thought would be a nice fresh leaf green has turned out more like neat limejuice? All these problems can be easily dealt with, Cinderella. The people who sell paint, especially the mix-on-the-spot varieties, are usually bored stiff with ringing up £4.99 for Brilliant White Gloss, and are also usually trained to know things like dark colours lower a high ceiling and a matt surface will recede more than a gloss one; if you talk to them, you may well find you are almost doing them a favour by getting them to experiment with different bases to find exactly the right match for your wallpaper sample, or discuss the peculiar requirements of the half embrasure beside the fireplace. But never ask their advice on colours – you don't know their tastes and they don't know yours. Your friends will be more than pleased to air their opinions too (an eye for colour is a *very* Superwoman characteristic), but again, do be careful to stick to asking those with the same sort of taste as yourself: Helen may be the smartest person you know, but you wouldn't like a cavern of dramatic scarlet and black if you're really a dimity and pastel person, or vice versa. You could even send off the inevitable small fee to one of the glossies to design a complete room scheme for you if you're really stuck, but once more, you don't know that the home editor thinks the same way as you do. The best general principle is to follow your own inclinations and only ask advice on how to achieve the desired effect, not on what that effect should be.

And as for the decorating labour itself – if in doubt, pay somebody. It's not worth making a botch of a lot of expensive materials for the sake of a few extra pounds or your amour-propre. But most decorating jobs are in fact not terribly difficult if they're taken slowly and in an orderly manner, and some of them are even quite enjoyable (I like painting door frames and laying carpets, which is lucky, because everyone else seems to hate them). And the ones you can't do or don't like – well, it shouldn't be beyond you to persuade 'Him' that they'll relax him at the weekend after the cerebral cares of the office – you'll just have yourself to blame if he makes more of a mess of them than you would have. Given the actual ability to achieve it, decorating also doesn't take very long if you can just devote a whole day – but that does mean a *whole* day, not what's left over from the regular chores – to do it in. You'll then need another whole day when the first coat's dry, or the wallpaper has settled or the carpet is delivered, but it's still better than a week of wallpaper paste on every light switch and a taste of white spirit in all the food.

Above all, in every sphere of your responsibilities, you may have to keep reminding yourself that it is *your* home and *your* life. You may be stuck with the nappies and the broom for some of the time, but you don't have to chain yourself to them and throw away the key. It's never going to look like Ideal Home for more than two minutes at a time – nothing ever can once you let humans into it, let alone children and animals – and if it did you would probably be thoroughly uncomfortable; your home, after all, is supposed to be a reflection of your personality, not your own private Forth Bridge. If you still feel you aren't able to manage it to a standard you can accept, what with the children, the dog, the gerbils and your Meals on Wheels, maybe you could afford some help? Or more help? If you can't, could you recruit your family (I assume that you're already exacting some assistance from them, not making a rod for your own back by waiting on them hand and foot: if not, why not?)? If you are already doing all these things and still can't cope – really *cope*, not achieve the impossible – then you are either hopelessly disorganized, hopelessly lazy and lying to yourself, hopelessly over-ambitious, or simply kidding yourself for some reason of your own. Whichever it is, you might as well give in gracefully, and accept that you were never designed to be a Superhousewife. Console yourself with your exquisite petit point, your sparkling car maintenance or your first-class degree in Higher Mathematics, and resign yourself to living in a cheerful muddle rather than a miserable one.

So now you're satisfied with your status and your housekeeping standards as well, but you still don't like it. In fact you find it all so boring you already get through the lot in half an hour a day, have taught the two-year-old to speak Spanish, and spend the rest of your time feeling thoroughly ill-used and unfulfilled; or you're so bored you can't bring yourself to do anything at all except to feel thoroughly . . . Yes, well. Once again, I'm afraid, you do exactly the same as Superwoman does, and 'pursue your own interests'. But your *own* interests is exactly what that means – not whatever form of self-improvement the press are extolling this week. If you were secretly delighted to leave a dead-end job when you had Jonathan but are bored now, then you really mustn't feel honour-bound to go back to it to help them out by doing part-time work at home, or you will only be exchanging one boredom for another. On the other hand if you love your work but can't go back, then if you can do it from home, do; even if it means hiring a babysitter while you shut yourself in the bedroom to get on with it. You don't have to go and learn Italian because it seems more sensible, when what you really want to do is rock-climbing, and the worst idea I've ever heard is taking a course so you can talk intelligently to your partner about his job – that way you really do lay yourself open to patronage at best and, at worst, instant strangulation.

If you don't intend to, or can't, keep up with some element of your pre-housewife career, then the obvious starting points for new interests outside the home are self-education, sport, and voluntary work. You can almost certainly find something that interests you in your area, whether it's Ancient Greek or marathon running, and there is definitely something that needs volunteers, whether the hospital library trolley or visiting old age pensioners; and if you're lucky enough with whatever you take up you'll also find some congenial friends, so you will have fulfilled a double purpose, because although your social life can't occupy your mind the whole time, you could do with having it for some of the time. But whatever activity you go in for, you must be careful not to let it become a drudgery itself rather than an escape from drudgery, so if you're bored stiff by the second lesson, or find that your practice or homework have become the same sort of chore as cleaning the windows or making Jemima's costume for the school play, then stop it. You may not be the sort of person who needs the discipline of a set course or routine to motivate yourself; you may even be the sort for whom discipline simply prevents you from enjoying anything at all, in which case you could follow up an ambition of your own. Reading the whole of Dickens, say, or taking the advanced driving test, or improving your backhand, doesn't have to conform to anyone's timetable but your own, and doesn't leave you with the sensation of having leapt determinedly out of one rut straight into another.

If you are planning to work from home, either almost immediately or at some point in the future, or if you want to start working at something new, you *must* set aside time for that and that alone. If your job is outside the home it will be easy enough, but there's no future in the belief that your home-knit sweater industry will get off the ground if it has to compete with the toddler, the washing-up and the laundry. Chores can be left until later, doors and telephones unanswered, or you can agree with a home help to deal with them – even one or two mornings a week will often give you the necessary base of working time. And children, as long as they have some adult supervision in case of disasters, can be shut out more easily than you might imagine. A friend of mine hires a childminder for the day and resolutely shuts her ears to the howls while she does translation work behind the closed dining-room door; in my family we knew perfectly well that only broken limbs or earthquakes were sufficient reason for braving the barricades on our journalist mother's deadline days, and I don't remember us ever resenting it.

The important thing is, whatever you're going to do with it, to have that time of your own anyway: whether you use it to write a bestselling novel, set up a thriving accountancy business, or collect stamps. The housewife suffers badly enough from the lack of private space – because the whole house is in a sense her territory, no part of it is ever exclusively so – without lacking time of her own as well. Even if you only set aside an hour a day which is yours and sacrosanct, and even if you spend it falling asleep over the first chapter of your latest library book, you have to convince yourself not to feel guilty about 'wasting' that time – because that hour is your very own time *to* waste if you want to. But do explain to your family first: both men and children are quick to accept it as your right if they know what you're doing, but get easily bewildered and hurt when you explode without warning because they need you to look at this or mend that the first minute you've sat down.

I know, you've heard it all before and it's all so predictable and not at all your scene. But something must be (unless your office job was the be-all and end-all of your existence, in which case I'd be surprised if you hadn't gone back to it, or transferred all your energies to home-making). Nobody is asking you to improve yourself, either intellectually or through 'good works' – just to interest yourself. You might make a small fortune knitting sweaters, or a much smaller one typing address labels, or spend one amassing the world's largest collection of stuffed mice. You might discover you're a brilliant artist, or a terrible actor, or a reliable Bingo caller at charity bazaars; you might take up chess one week and spend the next practising handstands – it simply doesn't matter *what* you do with your life, as long as it *is* your life and you're enjoying it, not feeling guilty that you aren't scrubbing the kitchen floor instead.

And before going on to look at your probable reason for being 'only a housewife' at all – motherhood – bear in mind that like all jobs, housewifery is frequently dull. But it is, like all the others, just a job; you, with your Superskills, can rise above it. After all, you could be stuck with something *really* boring, like advertising soap powder to housewives . . .

# 5
## *Madonna and Child*

That ugly, crude rather rude pottery statue of a huge-bellied and all too obviously female form which Steve brought you as a joke souvenir from his Far East trip is, of course, a primeval Earth Mother image. The joke, though, is that so – if less blatantly – are you. You are (presumably) a woman, and woman as mother is the most central, enduring and universal image in the human experience, ranging across all civilizations and all ages from the original of your pottery figure, via the Christian idealization of the Virgin with child, right the way forward to the Greenham women demanding a safe world for their children, and including you along the way. Not only is motherhood a basic genetic imperative, but it is the one thing a woman can do that a man can't do at all, let alone better; for centuries it has been the *only* thing that a woman could acceptably do, all her housewifely and hostly virtues being merely extensions of, or compensation for, this one: therefore you are a primeval fertility image whether you like it or not, and it will hardly surprise you that Ideal Motherhood is high on Superwoman's list of priorities for your attention.

Superwoman blossoms as a mother. Whether she has the average 2.1 children or a whole rambling brood, she devotes herself to them wholeheartedly from the first moment of conception to the devastating day when they become grown-ups. She is radiantly and proudly pregnant in vivid, bulge-emphasizing dungarees; meticulous in avoiding alcohol or incautious diet, she attends her exercise classes and practises her breathing religiously, prepares a nursery and layette that will do justice to her superbaby, and organizes the practicalities of birth, having read up all the right books and asked friends 'who know', well in advance. She carries the prints from her scan in her purse, and shows them to everyone who'll look; the time, place and circumstances in which she felt the first kick are etched on her memory; the birth itself, accomplished according to the most fashionable method of the moment – with father in attendance, possibly taking photographs or even, horror of horrors, a video – is the most indescribably wonderful experience anyone has ever known. The child is both beautiful and good, falling easily into a routine which allows her to remain radiant and organized throughout the hazards of four-hourly feeds, weaning, teething and potty-training; it hardly ever cries, very quickly learns to sleep through the night and take solid foods, and goes on until it's walking at six months and an intellectual prodigy at two. Superwoman's nanny, if she has one, is a treasure and the children adore her, but she is never in danger of supplanting their mother in their affections – who could supplant Superwoman as recipient of all troubles and purveyor of all physical and mental nourishment? She shares everything with her family and does everything for them up to the point when she instinctively knows they need to cope alone. She makes wonderfully shaped and decorated cakes for their birthday parties, which are always wonderfully organized; she nurses them tenderly through measles and the first days of school; she washes gym kits and chauffeurs them to school events and friends' houses without complaint; she decorates their rooms for stimulation and enjoyment at every stage of their development; she encourages their nascent genius with carefully chosen toys and books (and is careful, too, to play and read with them): it goes without saying that she is permanently feeding them. They confide all their worries to her and ask her advice about everything from their maths homework to their clothes; they bring their friends home to be included in her generous maternal embrace; they treat her as a friend and confidante and are proud of her at Speech Days. Yet she never smothers them, respects their privacy, weathers the storms of teenage rebellion with patience and tact and has the wisdom to let them go when they are ready to, thereby ensuring that they will always come back. Needless to say, her children grow up hard-working, handsome, charming, sensitive and responsible, and neither they nor Superwoman ever have a moment's cause to worry over the images of motherhood which have brought this happy state of affairs about.

In fact, the images of motherhood are rarely questioned; it is the one female attribute that everybody from male chauvinist pig to radical feminist (even if she's rebelling against it) takes for granted as the ultimate ideal for a woman. And yet the mystic aura of the Earth Mother which gives motherhood ideal status was bestowed upon us by men, to get over their embarrassment at not being able to emulate us – and if it is now extolled by women as well, that's largely to cover up *our* embarrassment at continuing to enjoy fulfilling a role we've loudly dismissed as one of servitude and second-class citizenship. The whole social condition of women has been defined over the centuries in such a way as to help men come to terms with our motherhood; the argument goes something like this: 'Since I owe my existence to woman's reproductive capacity, it must be significant. On the other hand, since only women have it, it can't possibly be as important as anything I can do; besides, it involves all sorts of demeaning unpleasantnesses, like physical pain, and blood, and cleaning up nappies, and it's very limiting, tying one down in one place unable to go off hunting, or off to war, or to discover space. This is exactly what you'd expect for the inferior sex, but the actual ability to give birth is a bit confusing – it must have some mysterious spiritual quality, which will account for me not being able to do it when as far as mere humans go I'm so clearly superior in every way. In which case I will accord suitable deference to women as the mortal vessels of the mystery of life, but just to make sure they don't get hold of the idea that gives them something I haven't got I will make it quite clear that their motherhood is only a significant quality in that men need mothers so we can exist and be free to rule the world – that should cover it.' Women, being more pragmatic and less competitive, besides being busy getting on with it, didn't need to idealize motherhood at all until we began insisting we were different from men: before that, women had babies, and the babies grew up either to rule the world or to have more babies to grow up and rule the world, and that was just the way things were: but all the same, it was nice to be granted a mystique to compensate for our inferiority, even if we were only the priestesses and the accolade was universal to all women and therefore low on the Brownie points.

It isn't quite as simple as that, of course. The real mystery and wonder we feel at our capability of giving life to another human being, which breathes and cries and has toes and fingers, does rather put motherhood on a different plane from any other activity. 'The moment you see your first child (and indeed your second and third and on up to your tenth or more, I daresay) is one of such overwhelming and joyful humility, such tender and dazzling happiness, that you realize everything you ever did or knew or had before counts for almost nothing at all' claims Penny Vincenzi (*Options*, March 1984). 'It is a physical invasion of love and like no other; it takes hold of your heart and does not let it go again . . . we may well discover in motherhood the most truly important thing we have ever done.' And there's lots more in the same vein; she is quite clearly in an advanced state of Supermotherhood which, while entirely enviable and no doubt admirable, doesn't make the problems of our Madonna image any simpler for anyone except other Supermothers.

As a would-be Superwoman you may be just as well aware of your mystic role as potential vessel for new life as Superwoman is, but since, unlike Superwoman, you are multi-dimensional, you can't just launch yourself into perfect motherhood regardless of its effect on the rest of your existence. Your career, your man, your social life, your finances, don't all live in separate pigeon-holes, never to meet your motherhood except in passing, but are continuously interreacting with it: living life in the round, you are faced with the necessity for compromise and the possibility of choice, and every choice you take leaves a residue of guilt over the one you rejected. And the problem is particularly acute because we are the first generation to be offered any real choice over motherhood at all – and scientific advances and social flux have coincided with our new freedom to offer us not one choice, but a whole bewildering range of them all at once.

You can choose whether to have children at all, and if so, how many and when – you can even choose whether your children will have two parents or, with a little AID from your friends, just one. You can carry a test-tube foetus, or your child can be carried by a surrogate mother. You can conduct your pregnancy in any number of ways, and choose from an enormous spectrum of conflicting theories on the manner of its birth. You can breast-feed it for months in expensive restaurants or the House of Commons, or leave it with a bottle and a nanny after a matter of weeks; and after this a succession of choices as to its upbringing hits you daily for the foreseeable future. At every turn you will be offered, frequently forcibly, a barrage of contradictory advice from all sides – after all, everyone has either given birth or been born, and therefore knows much more about it than you do; at every corner you will be temporarily panic stricken by the magnitude of your decisions, and your only certainty about them will be that they're wrong. As all women are presumed to be fertile unless proved otherwise, you don't even have to be a would-be Superwoman to fall into this particular trap, though you're more likely to if you are, since you will have more conflicting ambitions to contend with yourself before you start on the conflicting theories of everyone else: you're not conditioned for the responsibility of choice on this level, which makes your position eminently guilt-inducing. No wonder women are suffering increasingly from stress.

The first decision you have to make, once you question your automatic priesthood of Motherhood with a capital M, is whether you want to be a mother at all. Physically, with effective contraception freely available, it would be very easy not to once you'd made the choice (though the Pill, the coil and most other contraceptive devices raise guilt-inducing questions of their own), but to make the choice at all is much more difficult. The pressure of social expectation and persuasion is none the less for being frequently unwitting, or for existing in your own mind as well as the minds of your mother, your media mentors and your happily-mothering contemporaries: our society may not, as Germaine Greer claims, like children, but we are still enthralled by the idea of them – which makes it very hard for you to state baldly, either to yourself or to your best friend and mother of four, that you don't want to have any. Nobody actually thinks that they are being intrusive and irresponsible in urging you to have a child on the spurious grounds that 'your father would like to have grandchildren', or because human life is so sacred that you should embrace motherhood for the rest of yours as punishment for a moment of folly, or because 'it's so selfish not to' (though if you ask what's so selfless about having children, there's never a satisfactory answer): this is because nobody actually thinks about it at all, being so long conditioned in the belief that that's what every woman wants anyway. 'There is no yearning like that of a woman for a child' states Penny Vincenzi, without qualification or explanation: and we accept automatically that it is true for all women and all children.

And so the game goes on, and the minute you acquire a regular partner everyone from your mother to the office junior wants to know when you're getting married; as soon as the day is named, they're eager to have a timetable for the pregnancy too; the day you get back from your honeymoon they've got their magnifying glasses out looking for a tell-tale thickening of your waistline, and counting on their fingers to check whether gastric 'flu could be morning sickness; if these lines of enquiry frustrate them they will soon start muttering darkly about 'leaving it a bit late'. If you try to tell them that you're not only not pregnant but don't intend to be either they won't believe you anyway, but greet your defiance with a knowing smile and a 'You just wait . . .' and you will probably secretly think that they might be right – and they might at that. And since motherhood *is* still the one great success story of not only the female sex but the whole human race and animal kingdom to boot, you will add to the social pressure the sneaking suspicion that without it you've failed to make the required grade of womanhood, never mind Superwomanhood, which allows you to feel inadequate; the element of morality implicit in your mystical self-immolation on the altar of Birth makes you feel guiltily immoral if you avoid being the sacrifice. In effect, your choice is reduced to heads I win, tails you lose – you *can* take either of two decisions, but only one will be recognized as right.

You would have to be fairly tough to brazen it out against the weight of centuries of opinion, reinforced by your modern dream leader Superwoman, without succumbing to a certain amount of guilt and uncertainty about your isolated position out on your limb, and you would have to be very much more than usually analytical to develop a solid rational argument with which to answer it. You may very well not have addressed the question at all. But if women can continue to bear children on the startlingly unreasonable grounds they do, you can *not* bear them without having to justify your position any more reasonably: our attitudes to childbirth are emotional rather than logical. Any hesitation on your part surely shows that you are being both moral and responsible by giving the matter some thought – Superwoman ought to approve of *that*. And remind yourself, probably for the thousandth time, that the whole purpose of the revolution Superwoman's supposed to be leading is to win you the freedom to make your own choices; it may not help you to be certain you've made the right one, but at least it might help you to believe you had a right to make it.

If you are happily decided in favour of motherhood, however, your problems are only just beginning. The decisions lying in wait for you once you are actually and inexorably pregnant are immensely complicated and seem to go on virtually forever; the first of these, after you've given up smoking and drinking but before you've weighed up the relative merits of Le Boyer and National Health, or made a shortlist of names, will probably be whether or not you're going to carry on working. At this point you might get an unwelcome shock when your husband discovers you never intended to give up your job, or when you discover that he'd never considered the possibility you wouldn't (this is the sort of minor detail where fundamental differences in attitude emerge, but which quite often doesn't get thought about until it happens, and it has happened to friends of mine who I thought would have been more organized about their lives.) In fact a very high proportion of women, even women with fulfilling and potentially progressive careers, still abandon their salaried employment like a hot potato when motherhood beckons; whether because they genuinely want to devote themselves to their family; or because they feel they ought to, at least while the children are young, so they don't miss out on important bonding processes or intellectual stimulus; or because they work in positions which can't by their nature be made to dovetail with a demanding domestic schedule. But more and more women are continuing to work, despite the hideous reams of paperwork involved in doing so, and more and more employers are beginning to see the folly of losing highly trained and competent staff if they can possibly avoid it. Many employers, on the other hand, still covertly regard your pregnancy as an affront to the great god Mammon, and just the sort of thing a woman *would* do; they can't say so openly, of course, but if you suddenly find someone's set up a series of worried meetings when you've only just announced the happy news to discuss what rescheduling will be necessary when you come back from maternity leave, look out for the signs that you're gradually being persuaded you won't be able to cope! In Japan, a woman's male colleagues start giving her definite encouragement to get married when she reaches her late twenties, and almost no woman returns to work after the wedding, let alone the christening; not only does this relieve the men of one rival to their promotion, but it saves them having to face the potential traumas of working for a female superior – an idea that seems to strike terror into their hearts. (The friend who told me this didn't know of any man who'd actually gone so far as to marry a female colleague in the logical pursuit of this end, but I daresay they'll come to it in time.) And though we're well past the stage of such sexual paranoia in the West, there can still be a persistent subconscious prejudice against working mothers on the grounds that they are disruptive of the smooth, single-minded flow of business even more than non-mother women are; this attitude isn't confined to men, either. A highly intelligent and highly-trained friend of mine, working in a specialized field for a company who do have a good reputation for retraining and so retaining female staff after maternity leave, astonished me recently by announcing that she thought it was unfair on the company to expect them to keep her job open for her, and I don't suppose for a moment she is alone.

If you don't give up your job, you will almost immediately discover that the bureaucratic processes of pregnancy and birth for the working woman were designed to make you regret your decision. The level of maternity benefit may vary from company to company, but the complexity and volume of forms seems to be universal. So while you're yo-yoing between the physical and mental highs and lows, contending with the highly charged emotional confusion into which your physical state has thrust you, and 'making sure your work doesn't suffer' from this invasion of the rest of your life, you will also be called upon to grapple with mountains of impertinent questions about your medical history, and unanswerable ones about your post-natal intentions and probable state of health. Your mathematical skills will have to be finely tuned to a standard only marginally sub-genius, since some of those forms have managed to get themselves worded in such a way that they allow room for your entire benefit to be forfeit if you're a week out with the projected birthdate, so have your calendar and calculator synchronized and pray for an uncomplicated delivery. To be fair, I've never actually heard of anyone invoking the invalidity clause, which suggests that it isn't part of a deep-laid plot against us but merely incompetence – but the possibility, however remote, that an unscrupulous employer *could* is one more worry you can probably do without at the moment. And if you're finding it difficult to make up your mind whether you want to return to work or not, you'll get no help from the hard-pressed administrators: those forms need definite answers, and they need them now – besides, the firm itself will be itching to swing into action on either recruitment or temporary cover for you, and a silly woman who won't make up her mind doesn't get a lot of sympathy when there's money at stake.

The actual choice, whether to work or not to, will probably seem easy to start with and get more difficult as you go along – motherhood really does change your life, and all your formerly ordered imperatives with it. It's not that anyone is really callous or indifferent to your problems, but the ramifications of them are so new and various that nobody, not even you, actually understands what they are. Your man will almost certainly try very hard to come to grips with an idea of what you want, and then support you in aiming for it, but he will be as baffled as your personnel department when every time you seem to have made a decision you promptly produce a string of counter-arguments to it, and while he, like Superwoman, can clearly comprehend practical considerations, he will be confused and embarrassed by the contradictory, illogical emotions behind your vacillations, and finally, if you go on too long, simply bored. Your family and friends will no doubt offer you reams of advice, given from a position of either ignorance or their own choices, already made; Superwoman herself will bombard you with totally contradictory theories and plans of action at the drop of a hat. Ultimately, however, you come down to the fact that the most difficult decisions of your life will always have to be made by you and you alone, which does after all seem perfectly fair.

Once you've negotiated the pre-natal administrative minefield, and opened, with suitable cries of delight, the stylish candy-striped Babygro and the hand-knitted matinee jacket, you set off to wait at home in splendid isolation for the imminent social and medical tyranny that surrounds childbirth itself to take you over. Since the various options available for birth itself have been, and are, endlessly discussed and written about, you will already be well aware of their various advantages and disadvantages, and there's no need to go into them here: the merits of home versus hospital, 'natural' versus male-dominated clinical births, the mysticism of bonding, and the probable desirability or otherwise of retiring to a matriarch-run crèche for a couple of years are all topics with which would-be Superwomen tend to be familiar, and which you will no doubt have spent the first months of your pregnancy anxiously revising. The theories come, and either go or stay; they tend to be conflicting and are sometimes mutually exclusive, and are all in any case old dogma or anthropological borrowings dressed in new ideologies; most of them probably contain a grain of truth and a grain of nonsense, and none of them should be taken as gospel: all that matters is to find – if you can in this maze – the solution that works best for you and ignore all the others.

Most of the literature, however, concentrates on the

physical aspects of pregnancy and birth, with a large injection of mysticism in relation to the central, magical experience of birth and the subsequent mysteries of the bonding process, which in some doctrines gets a formula as precise and inhuman as that for any Superglue. (In fact, very like Superglue: carefully clean and prepare surfaces to be bonded; position in contact, apply gentle pressure and do not disturb for x minutes – read mother and baby for 'surfaces' and you're almost exactly there.) Unlike Superwoman, however, the rest of us can't expect the world or even the rest of our own lives to come to a grinding halt so we can treat childbirth as a separate, unconnected event; life isn't like that. Germaine Greer is one of the very few feminist apostles to recognize, or at least point out, that childbirth is not a magic bubble in which mother and baby are cocooned in splendid isolation, and on which no such trivia as our needs and emotions outside this one event impinge. She highlights, rather, the sense of alienation felt by a woman uprooted from her peer group at a time when she most needs the support of their company; the crisis of self-confidence for the career woman reduced in status to mother; the affront to her intelligence, her individuality and her self-esteem when she is subjugated to the priests and technicians of birth for all the world as if it were none of her business. All of which is true, and the fact that Germaine Greer rather strangely seems to suggest that a different style of female bondage would solve the problem doesn't invalidate her recognition of motherhood as part of the larger context of life.

But even she is dealing in theories, and doesn't reach as far as the all-pervading, guilt-ridden counterbalance of alternatives involved in the whole business – and once again, every decision you make will be wrong. If you obey your traditionalist doctor and are delivered lying on your back waving your legs in the air and gritting your teeth, you are reneging on your neo-Earth Mother image, and are no doubt causing untold physical trauma to your child; if you squat screaming in a corner you'll be upsetting all your own social conditioning by flouting authority and 'calling attention to yourself', and may risk increased physical trauma through untold complicated emergencies – as the midwife said tartly, 'Where am I supposed to be, lying on the floor?'. If you persuade John to be present at the birth, he's just as likely to be more of a strain than a comfort to you, but if you don't, you'll be depriving him of his share in the bonding process, and he'll be evermore unglued. And so on, and so on – once again there are too many options available to you for the first time to make your decision anything but impossible, which seems very unfair when there are quite enough physical and psychological traumas to cope with in the birth process already without taking on the added goals of Supermotherhood. And yet it is encouraging to see that women today face all of them with an astonishing degree of success and lack of drama: as next year's fad supplants this year's, only to be superseded by the one after that, women continue to have babies in enormous numbers and an enormous variety of circumstances, and by and large they survive both the experience and the fad. It might just be possible that you could do the same . . .

So somehow you have weathered the conflicting pressures and sensations of the perinatal period, and now you're back home with this extraordinary, demanding object that wields the most phenomenal power over you simply by being so very vulnerable, and of which you are about to discover that 'the baby's power to transform you from person to mother is almost mystical in its strength' (Penny Vincenzi). In the next few weeks you are going to learn a routine acceptable to yourself, your man, and to the small monster now overriding both of you; discover things about all your characters you'd never dreamed of; suffer from boredom, exhaustion, frustration, post-natal depression and blind panic; find out about mothering; readjust to your altered physical image, and come to terms with the alterations in others' images of you; change your mind a hundred times a day about going back to work; check every half-hour that it's still breathing; develop an unsqueamish stomach, an ability to go without sleep, and your muscles; understand that from now on everything's going to take at least twice as long as it used to; become besotted with baby-sized fingernails and obsessed with germs; love it passionately and cease to have any independent existence yourself – which is the chief problem you'll have to sort out when your feet hit the ground again.

The trouble is that once you set out to be a mother at all, and particularly a Supermother, you almost necessarily give up being a person – or at least everyone else seems to assume you do. Having faithfully followed Superwoman all this way in the optimistic belief that you are an individual with several equally important areas of existence and achievement, you suddenly find that she's led you into a cul-de-sac, where your talents as a trapeze artist, an accountant, a cook, a squash player, and certainly as a lover or even an attractive woman, are mutually exclusive with your motherhood. Katharine Whitehorn goes even further in describing your depersonalization, and claims you become 'a place to be crawled over like an outcrop of rock, a place to come home to . . . you're just an aspect of themselves, with very little independent existence' (*Observer*, 1.4.84), and even in the throes of her enthusiasm Penny Vincenzi admits that a baby can impose on its mother a kind of 'emotional solitary confinement'. Motherhood is such a pinnacle of achievement for you (remember?) that everything else, even attributes that couldn't possibly interfere with it, like your virtuoso tap dancing, pales into significance and gets swallowed up in it almost at once; you may have escaped from the days when you existed only as a back-up life support system for your man, but you're still stuck with it for your children.

This 'emotional solitary confinement' is heightened by the physical isolation you are necessarily subjected to as soon as you have a baby to contend with – and even if you're going back to your job in three months' time, three months is quite long enough to crack up in. All humans need stimulus from their peers, and since even mothers have now been classified as more or less human that goes for you too. But an inarticulate bundle of baby clothes is not your peer, and although it can at times be stimulating to preside over and share in its development it is equally often tiring, lonely and boring. But because you're now a mother, not a person, that is your accepted lot; nobody will understand that you could still want to be a trapeze artist too. 'Could people please stop assuming that because we can – or could – do motherhood, we therefore can't do anything else?' demands Katharine Whitehorn. 'You say a man's a good father . . . it certainly doesn't imply that this is all he does. Yet "she's a good mother" suggests that she has no other existence.'

And of course you haven't. You are now, to all intents and purposes, exactly the same creature as 'only a housewife', and you will have to make the same compromises and the same efforts as she does to ensure that you keep at least a corner of your individuality for a rainy day or when you're allowed to be a person again. Whatever myths Superwoman may have perpetuated, they're still myths, and however firmly tied your umbilical cord, it needn't be a leash but only a safety rope: you are still a separate person as well as a mother, and your only hope of being a happily confident one is to keep reminding yourself of it.

If you are going back to work, you needn't think you've escaped the Trap just by making that decision. At eight o'clock one morning, far too soon, you'll be rooted at the front door (because your knees won't work) clutching your briefcase in one hand and one of your baby's precious fingers in the other, convinced that without your restraining presence the nanny will be transformed into a baby-batterer or pyromaniac, and the baby is only waiting for you to get out of sight before going into strong convulsions, and you've forgotten everything you ever knew about overnight borrowing anyway – and generally feeling about as much like Superwoman as a wet nappy. Contrary to anything you may have been led to believe, this is perfectly normal; and the more organized and business-like you've been up to now, the less rein you've given to your wilder nightmares and emotional absurdities, the more normal it is. The idea of abandoning your helpless innocent to the tender mercies of Another fills you with phenomenal terror and raging guilt, largely because it is natural for a woman to want to be with her child.

Well actually, it isn't. In Western society, at least, the idea of woman and child being constantly in each other's sole company is as new and strange as that of combining your roles as careerwoman, wife and housekeeper; today's revisionist who cries 'You should be at home looking after your children' completely forgets that when a woman *was* at home, she was rarely looking after her children. Just as she instructed the housekeeper, and did the flowers or made some special dish herself, so she consulted with the nanny or governess, and spent an hour or so with the children; beyond that the nursery/schoolroom world operated more or less independently of the adult. And the children of grander establishments were frequently sent away at an early age to be brought up in another household altogether, not to see their parents again until adulthood. A working woman left her children in whatever care she could find, if any; if she were tied to them, and so not free to work, they were all quite likely to end up in the poorhouse, and if they were with her all day it was only because they were working in the same field or mill to add their few pence to the family income. And don't believe all the myths about more primitive societies either – what about all those weaklings left out on the hillside to die, the seven-year-old boys taken off to live with the men, the young girls chosen amid general rejoicing for sacrificial or other less terminal mystic rites? It was only when World War Two evened up the classes and the sexes that a generation made a virtue out of necessity be deciding it was 'natural' to act out their days in Superwoman's neo-Earth Mother role.

Which doesn't mean to say that you're wrong, in the light of today's more open, warmer family relationships, to disapprove of the former regimented and distant attitude to children shown by the better off, or of the joyless hardships they and their parents suffered if they were poor: just that you'd be wrong to let Superwoman con you into feeling guilty for being unnatural. We confuse the separateness of attitude with the physical separateness of time and place, and assume that we must be guilty of our ancestors' coldness because the only precedent we have for families who spent large chunks of their time apart is those who subscribed to that coldness; there are no role models to show us how to differentiate between the two. Yet you don't have to be with your man, or your best friend, or your mother every hour of the day and night to have a close and loving relationship with them – so why should you with your children? Certainly not because there is any long-standing tradition of a suffocatingly close mother-child relationship to affirm it.

Far from it harming little Miranda's psyche if you go back to work and leave her with a carefully-picked, responsible person who has chosen a career looking after children because she (usually she) likes it and is good at it, you are saving both her and yourself from the risks of smother-love and stultifying boredom. Your child needs intellectual stimulus as much as you do – more, since he or she can't be expected to find it within – and no two people constantly in each other's company will get much mental excitement out of the arrangement. A child also needs to be presented with a range of people in order to discover that such things exist; as Miranda grows up, the diversity provided by even a mere two female authority figures will stand her in good stead when she takes on the external authority of school or play-group, and you wouldn't want her to disgrace you by being a Mummy's girl, would you? Besides which, you may not be very good at caring for children, nor very happy doing it, especially if you're yearning in your heart for the buzz of the dealing room, and it is surely only common sense to see that a child will be happier with someone who is happy herself than with a discontented misery who is there for no other reason than a perceived biological necessity?

You may, of course, be blissfully happy being a Supermother, and not even guilty of smother-love or suffering (much) from boredom either. In which case, there is no reason to feel that you're letting down Supercareerwoman by kissing your directorship goodbye without a twinge of regret: somebody else will be around to look after that image, as if it needed it. The freedom to stay at home through choice, rather than through social acceptability, is one that really *has* come into its own, and if you're happy doing it the slings and arrows of the career snobs will glance off you. But you will have to watch out – as will your careerist counterpart – for any signs of smugness or righteousness over your choice: neither of you is right or wrong, and either way you're luckier than your predecessors in simply being allowed to *make* a choice.

Just as childbirth doesn't happen in isolation from the rest of your life, so it can't be isolated from thc problems of children – which go on, and on, and on . . . This is not a manual of women's health, and nor is it about to rival Doctor Spock with a new theory of childcare. What suits you and your child will be anathema to somebody else, and vice versa, and every theory will always be tempered by inconsistency and pragmatism. Whatever you try to do, you won't be able to win: however much you may believe that by the time they can walk or talk you'll be free to be you again, you'll be proved wrong. Especially as they grow older, everything you are, say and do will be compared unfavourably with what Jimmy or Sarah's mother is, says and does: when they're no longer totally dependent on you for survival, they will occupy just as much of your time and attention, and even more of your space; when they're capable of eating without your help, you'll find you've only turned from a vending machine to an open-all-hours cafeteria waitress; when they abandon nappies, they acquire sports kits and impractical fashion garments; when you no longer have to bath them, you'll find them permanently occupying the bathroom – and all this will go on long after everyone but you has ceased to regard them as children at all. You will carry on making decisions – about their sex-stereotyping, their education, their pocket money, the decor of their bedrooms, the hour of their curfew, what to tell them about the divorce, when to call the doctor, when they're being sad, or just bad, when to put yourself before them and when not to – and you will carry on feeling guilty about the choices you've made and the ones you've rejected. And of course, just as there is no law that you have to like or be good at motherhood, there is certainly none that your children will appreciate you for it, or respond to the agonies you went through over your choices and decisions – and they won't. After all, why should they – they didn't have any choice in the matter at all.

And where does your man fit into all this? (I'm afraid I've been assuming that you are conventional or fortunate enough to have a partner in your childbearing; if not, then obviously he won't fit into it at all.) Up to now, throughout the months of pregnancy and the early stages of babyhood, he has probably fitted in more or less peripherally, and until our generation he would have continued to do so. But increasingly, he is finding it more and more difficult to formulate his role in this new society. However empathetic, fair-minded and female-orientated he is – and the majority of intelligent young men are all these things in abundance – his inbred attitudes to your several roles in life, and to your motherhood in particular, go as deep as your own, while your new celebration of the dominance of the Earth Mother confuses him even more by turning his own historical arguments against him. Moreover, he is less finely tuned than you are to the complexity of the multiple choices open to you today; he likes decisions to be black-and-white, clear-cut and simple, and would rather avoid them completely than have to make any that involve unpleasantness – but nothing in his life is clear-cut any more, and he's quite likely to be confused and cross about the whole set up. So that when you appeal to him for support over Jonathan's rudeness or Sally's over-hectic social life, he won't be any more help than he was over the two in the morning feed or the rash that might have been scarlet fever; he'll almost certainly back you up, but he won't, almost equally certainly, take an independent lead. This is the penalty you pay for promoting your Superwoman image: that your man will probably be more aware of your position and problems, but less able to help you through it, than at any other point in our history.

All in all, we're still in a pretty fair mess over motherhood, and haven't yet achieved any real freedom from its mystic bonds, let alone its practical shackles, whatever we try to believe or do about them: that must wait for the next generation or the one after that. But though there's still a long way to go, we've come some distance already, and it would be wrong to think that the message is gloom, doom and a sell-out on all sides: there are some distinct plus points. It may not be entirely socially acceptable yet for you to choose marriage without children, but it is at least physically possible, and choosing children without marriage, or even partnership, is certainly on the cards. It is also socially as well as legally possible for you to return to work if you want to, treating motherhood as one phase of your life rather than the be-all and end-all of it: gradually it is becoming both practicable and acceptable for you to hire the nanny who can make it a normal event, not a privilege reserved for the better-off or less socially conscientious. You can choose from any number of options as to the method and timing of your motherhood. And the option that has become the most acceptable of all is, funnily enough, the one that we've wrongly persuaded ourselves was always there, but as destiny not decision: that is, of course, 'traditional', 'natural' Earth-Motherhood . . .

# 6
# *The Perfect Hostess*

Entertaining is perhaps the pinnacle of Superwoman's achievement. When she issues you with an invitation – about three weeks before the day, not such short notice that you're likely to be booked up, nor so far in advance as to be over-formal or forgettable – you accept and sit back in happy anticipation of an excellent evening. Whether she is giving a party or a dinner, her favourite social enterprise, she will have left nothing to chance and made no mistakes. The right number of people for the style of occasion, carefully selected to be both compatible and stimulating, will turn up on time and on good form, ensuring that the social side of the evening runs smoothly and pleasantly without more than an occasional helping hand from Superwoman, and the catering will be of the highest possible standard.

If you're lucky enough to be asked to dinner, Superwoman either remembers, or knows by instinct, exactly what you want to drink, whether Tequila or tonic water, and has a glass of it ready even before you've taken off your coat, along with a selection of interesting nibbles from east of Suez. As you sit down and are introduced to a fellow guest you get on with immediately, you will have just the right length of time to admire her elegant and spotless decor in return for her compliments on your looks and interested enquiries after your or your family's latest exploits before she flits off to attend to another arrival or check something in the kitchen (where, she will assure you, everything is under control, and no, you can't do anything to help except sit down and *relax*). And when everyone has arrived and had time to unwind and get on easy terms with each other, you will all be shepherded gently into the dining room and directed unobtrusively to seats which have been carefully planned beforehand.

The candles match the table linen, which was practically designed for the room, and are set off by charming flower arrangements small enough not to obstruct your view of the people on the other side of the table and so interfere with the easy flow of conversation or access to the salt. The cutlery and crockery are complete sets too, twinkling at their reflections in the array of cut or Dartington glass: nobody will end up with the kitchen fork or the odd plate. The food, it goes without saying, is impeccable; top quality ingredients, perfectly cooked to highly complicated recipes – and you wouldn't be uniquely favoured if it ran to four courses with a choice of puddings and cheese to follow. The wine is good, if usually unadventurous, and there is Perrier for those who want it, with a selection of liqueurs, coffee and 'old-fashioned' mint chocolates back in the sitting room afterwards. You will never at any time feel you've outstayed your welcome or been persuaded towards the door, but it will be not long after midnight when you accept your coat and Superwoman your thanks – because she's going to be clearing and washing up while you're happily snuggling down to sleep in the warm afterglow of a delightful evening.

Superwoman's parties, whether for adults or children, are equally splendid. She works hard at them, and is rarely disappointed, for like *Look Now* she knows that 'you'll only get out of a celebration what you put into it . . . with party-planning, there's actually an awful lot at stake'. She usually provides a reason as a focus for the celebration, whether it's a birthday or Bastille Day, and where there is no theme inherent in the occasion she will frequently create one. It was almost certainly a Superwoman who first invented the fancy dress party, and devised the famous between-wars phenomenon of the 'red dinner' (colours make good themes, easily imposed and effectively all-embracing). In extreme cases, she spares no expense on hiring professional caterers, entertainers, furniture removers and dance-floors, and sometimes even security guards: this has the dual effect of saving her work and making her guests feel privileged. But she never makes the mistake of skimping on food and drink, or demanding uncomfortable costumes for the sake of authenticity, relying instead on her meticulous background organization and social talents to ensure that her guests will leave when she wants them to, just as contented as after one of her dinners. And needless to say, she is equally proficient at creating amusing and original picnics at the races, outings to the country and evenings at the theatre.

There is a marked difference between this vision of gracious living and entertaining as undertaken by the would-be Superwoman – if, indeed, you aren't too much of a Trap-ee to attempt entertaining at all. The would-be Superwoman starts off preparing for her dinner party with wonderful intentions, but without any certainty as to whether she is going to have a stupendous success or a slightly suspect mix of guests (and possibly even, horror of horrors, unbalanced numbers!) eating not quite delicious food on a day inconvenient for herself. She plans an elaborate menu, with each course carefully chosen to complement the others, and then finds at the last minute that the greengrocer's avocados are all hard, or the butcher has sold his last pork fillet, and she either has to compromise or start her planning all over again. She can never remember what she gave to whom last time they came, and goes through agonies over whether it was Maria or Julie who's allergic to shellfish, and can she possibly serve Coq au Vin to Louise and Harry when she's sure she gave it to them about three years ago? Either she spends three solid evenings beforehand cooking, or she gets caught out and has to shop in her lunch hour, then rush home to create a five-course Cordon Bleu effort in two hour flat, as well as cleaning up the flat, setting the table, changing her clothes and finding some make-up. The last two items often haven't been achieved by the time the guests arrive, and she will have to either abandon her visitors with nervously over-large drinks while she changes, or feel there's no point now they've already seen her in her office skirt and sweater: either way, she's failed already. Dinner will be later than she intended, because she didn't realize the sauce would take so long to thicken, or forgot to put the vegetables on, so everyone will be a little light-headed when they sit down ('Sorry about that chair, Gerald, it's all right if you don't move around too much') so perhaps they won't notice that she's using the kitchen cutlery and the vegetable dishes don't match. She will apologize for every dish even while she's being complimented on it, and will call attention in this way to failings nobody would ever have noticed otherwise: by the time the last guest has gone she is miserably tired, anxiously convinced they haven't enjoyed themselves, and could no more face the washing up than climb Everest.

Her parties follow much the same pattern, and since she also has a tendency to decide briskly one day that she must *do* something about her social life, and then tries to do it all at once, she may well end up with six dinner parties and one drinks party in the course of a month. After all this physical and nervous exhaustion, it's not very surprising that she can develop a full-blown panic at the very idea, and let her social life dwindle into extinction because after a while she simply can't even begin to imagine how she could conceivably cope with spaghetti for four unless she took the whole day off to prepare it.

Just because you can't attain Superwoman's exaggerated standards of hospitality, there's no need either to kill yourself trying or to give up completely: lower your standards. It's too easy to forget, in your frantic concern for the exact stage of brûlée to which you should grill the crême, that presumably you have invited your guests round because you like them, and want to spend a relaxed, enjoyable evening with them – but how can any of you relax if you insist on treating the whole occasion like a colour supplement cookery competition? Nobody wants to be intimidated by over-perfect food, just as I defy any ordinary person to *enjoy* drinking a wine when they know it costs £50 a bottle, or feel comfortable in a precisely-regimented, Ideal Home photograph, pale grey and white sitting room, drinking eminently spillable coffee out of translucent Sevres cups, or relaxed in a hot and heavy gorilla costume. Remember how much fun it all seemed in those far-off, first-flat sharing days, when everyone sat on the floor eating overcooked spaghetti off chipped and borrowed plates and drinking warm Italian wine from those two-litre bottles out of assorted tumblers? I'm not suggesting that you necessarily want to regress quite so far now you're a mature and sophisticated career woman, but the principle is there: it's the people and the mood that matter, not the material trappings.

It sounds obvious to suggest that when you're planning a dinner party you should start with the fundamental decision about who you want to invite, and invite them: but it happens that way less often than you might at first suppose. Too many dinners are based on a chain of compromises of such complexity that the end result is boringly uncomfortable: first the panic that you're falling behind in the hostess stakes and must have somebody round; followed by the arbitrary fixing of a date that's suitable for you and your man; followed by the point-non-plus when your first choice of guest can't make it, and a subsequent reworking of the entire cast; finally by the last-minute inclusion of your sister or neighbour, who won't get on with anybody but will balance up the numbers.

So first pick the one or two people you really want to see, then – assuming eight as a perfect number, and two of them being hosts – make a note of eight more people you would like to introduce your first choice to, or who will get on with them and are next in your category of people *you* want to see. Ring to invite your first choice for the date you have in mind, but if he or she can't make it have an alternative ready: there is no rule to say you have to have a dinner party on that particular day, but it would be silly to have it without the main reason for its existence. Only when you've got that date sorted out ring the others – and don't suggest alternative dates for those who can't come, or you'll end up with two dinner parties to plan instead of one; just put them to the top of your list for 'another time'. And if you can't get a full complement from your top league, don't go mad and start ringing frenziedly through your address book to make the numbers come out right. The numbers don't have to come out 'right'. Six is as good a number as eight; three congenial people will enjoy themselves as much as any even number; equally, there's nothing to say you can't add an old friend who's turned up from Alaska at the last minute to make it nine, as long as you haven't carefully counted out chops or chicken quarters, and even then you can make emergency extensions. And as for the desperate desire to even up the sexes – why, unless you're setting up to rival Dateline, does it matter?

Be ruthless, too, about that couple you met ten years ago and found boring then, but who keep asking you round so you've got to ask them back. You haven't. You have enough hassle entertaining the people you like without having to do it out of a sense of duty, and it's not fair on your other guests either; why should you inflict on them somebody you find boring, when they don't even share your real or imagined obligation for hospitality received? If you mildly like them, ask them to a party, or meet them for lunch, or arrange to go out for a film and a pizza with them instead; their company will be diluted and therefore not so boring, it won't put any demands on your other friends, and you won't resent them for causing you all that work on culinary miracles. Or you could confine yourself to taking flowers and a bottle of wine with you and sending a pretty thank-you postcard afterwards if you feel constrained to accept their invitations: your social obligations do not extend to twenty-pounds-worth of food and drink, a week's work, and a worry-filled, boring evening.

Once you've settled your cast of characters you can start worrying about what to feed them on – remembering, of course, that there are no prizes or even Brownie points on offer. Many a perfectly straightforward evening has been ruined by a misguided determination to outdo Carême. Sophie may make superb Charlotte Russe and Jonathan have a wonderful way with pheasant, but they don't necessarily want to be drawn into a competition; besides, Sophie sniffs all the time and Jonathan's a terrible snob, and you don't want to copy those characteristics, do you? Maybe they are better cooks than you are, or more impressive ones at least – but they've accepted your invitation, so presumably they aren't worried they're going to be poisoned, and maybe their enthusiasm over the phone wasn't just politeness, but they're genuinely looking forward to an evening with more to offer than an elaborate menu? Which doesn't mean to say you have to give them Shepherd's Pie (which I actually find takes a lot more effort than many much 'smarter' dishes anyway), but does mean that the sky isn't going to fall on your head if you can't get to grips with the three hours worth of haute cuisine per course or making your tomatoes look like waterlilies.

You may be an excellent, fast, cook who enjoys cooking, in which case you won't have any problems here. But speaking as a moderate cook, who only likes it in spontaneous bursts when I don't have to do it, but who does want to make an effort if only to show my friends I care, I've found that a certain amount of simple trickery can help to create a meal with flair quickly and easily. Firstly, work out the entire menu the weekend before, or at the very least two days beforehand: you can then have non-perishable ingredients ready bought and waiting in the larder, Superwoman-style, and have time to adapt to such unforeseen problems as a sudden dearth of ripe avocados or the difficulty of tracking down parsley in the winter. Base your meal firmly on a dish you know tastes good and you can cook with the minimum of angst (culinary experiments should only be tried on *very* good friends); it's then easy to decide on the trimmings to complete that particular course, whether it's Lyonnaise potatoes and new broccolli, or simply fresh granary bread or cream. The dish doesn't have to be haute cuisine, but it helps if it's particularly attractive to look at – a prawn and avocado salad, for instance, looks more special than avocado with prawns, or a goulash topped with sour cream and paprika than an ungarnished beef casserole, however delicious, and in both cases they take the same time to make. Alternatively, something can become a great success simply through varying the normal scale: individual moulds of mousse, say, or dishes of pasta, cost an extra minute of serving time but no more, and a chicken and mushroom pie for four is only a pie, while one for twelve is the eighth wonder of the world.

When you've chosen your main culinary event, design everything else to fit round it – in every sense. You can do without two recipes that need constant last-minute attention, or both need instant action the minute you fling yourself through the door. Ideally, you could have one course at least dealt with and out of the way the day before, or even if you're lucky or very well-organized, the previous weekend; another course that requires very little preparation, depending solely on good, fresh ingredients, and one that may need a certain amount of work but needs it at convenient times. Remember that really good food is best served as near to its natural state as possible, before you devise an elaborate menu that involves you in a week's work pulping and mixing away until nothing bears any resemblance to its origins.

Colour, texture and little touches can play all sorts of tricks for you too. You can get away with serving a green salad pretty welll straight if you serve it as a separate course 'to clear the palate', or avoid it being boring as part of a course by adding a couple of slices of orange and a handful of toasted pine kernels. Similarly, fresh fruit can't be beaten as a pudding – but dates, plums, and chinese gooseberries are more exciting than apples and oranges. And the 'little touches' make all the difference: you can turn Chilli con Carne from student fare to exotica, just by adding diced carrot and sultanas to the rice, and surrounding the whole with small individual dishes of cucumber in yoghurt, tomatoes with olives and basil, grated cheese, orange and watercress, and guacamole – again, it takes no more time than mixing them all together, but it looks so colourful and as if trouble has been taken that nobody will believe it is less than gourmet cuisine. And variety in colour and texture are vital: Crab Mousse, followed by Coronation Chicken, followed by cheesecake, however carefully you've made them, will all taste the same, because they all look the same and have soft creamy bases – so two thirds of your effort will have been wasted. Whereas a spinach tart, followed by Coronation Chicken, followed by a red fruit salad, will win you an almost completely undeserved culinary reputation, because the eye and the 'crunch factor' give the appetite an interest. (This particular combination is also incredibly quick and easy to prepare, so you'd win all ways round: and cheese-cake has been so ubiquitous for the past decade it's time everyone but Superwoman gave it a rest anyway.)

If you're really pushed for time, and if money isn't too much of a problem once in a while, the great stand-bys are the very expensive foods. It's by using these that so many single men acquire their reputations as master chefs: yet the amount, or expertise, of cooking required for smoked salmon, steak and a wide range of excellent cheeses is hardly taxing to anything but the wallet. And don't be put off by the idea that you're somehow cheating unless everyone can tell immediately how much labour of love has gone into their stomachs – wouldn't you like to be offered smoked salmon, or rare roast beef, or wild strawberries, or any of the other luxury foods you wouldn't dream of buying for yourself? Money may be a cheap way of showing you care, as they say, but it can be a delicious one too.

And one last thing before we get totally carried away on a foodie freak-out: if there is one dish you are particularly good at, enjoy making and enjoy eating, why ration yourself? In most would-be Superwomen's lives, dinner party guests are repeated too seldom to risk being bored by your Tarte aux Pommes Normande or your Salmon and Cucumber Mousse. Restaurants have Specialités de la Maison – there's no reason why you shouldn't too. In fact, if you can get four dishes, say, for each course, down to a fine art, there's no reason on earth why you shouldn't rotate them indefinitely. I have one generous friend who gives me blinis with smoked salmon and sour cream every time I go – the second time he did it by accident, but the enthusiasm was such that since then he's done it on purpose – and the wonderful glow of relaxed anticipation in the knowledge of a known culinary treat in excellent company lasts me from receipt of the invitation to the evening itself. The only time you need worry at all about whether you can give Mary *that* is if you're not sure about any allergies, in which case you should phone up and check rather than worrying about it; far better than getting it wrong and giving her mussels, or alternatively avoiding your favourite lobster permanently just in case.

Once you've ensured that you're going to spend the evening with the people you want to spend it with, and you'll be eating food you're confident of, your major worries are out of the way. But there remains the practical consideration of a full-time job, or full-time children, to be combined with the arduous business of shopping, peeling vegetables, cooking, and changing into an unruffled, smoothly-dressed hostess – all of them no doubt to be achieved in two hours flat if you're lucky.

Shopping is why you planned your menu at the weekend, and you've already done it, just as Superwoman would have, apart from the perishables. You might even have cooked or prepared some items, though unless you want to make a particular dish that you need to leave to marinate, or chill, or something, I generally don't think it's necessarily a good idea to do too much in advance: on the basis that work expands to fill all the time available to it, and that goes for cookery too, which means you risk spending three evenings cooking for 'the day', and instantly rule out any possibility of treating it as a relaxing, non-competitive way to spend an evening. But since you have ruthlessly reduced your dinner party repertoire to include only dishes you are confident of and can make quickly, that shouldn't upset you too much anyway. But do have the food there if you can, and do clear the kitchen completely the night before; then all you should be carrying when you come home from work on the dinner party day is fresh meat, fresh bread and dairy produce, and a large bunch of flowers if you remember and felt up to affording them.

As far as the state of the home is concerned, you should already have discovered by now that a mild disarray is not only perfectly acceptable, but even positively welcome. The precise geometrical distribution of sofa cushions will encourage all but the most confident visitors only to perch nervously on the edge of the seat for fear of disturbing them; if you polish the side table to within an inch of a skating rink and rush forward with coasters at the drop of a tonic-water bubble, or with dustpans at the drop of a Twiglet, you'll give everyone nervous dyspepsia before they've even looked at your Tarte aux Asperges garni de Saumon Fumé, never mind the rest of the courses; and by the time you've assured them that it really doesn't matter in the *slightest* that they've helpfully put the wrong chair at the foot of the table you'll be lucky if they dare eat anything at all, open their mouths, or move. Rooms are for living in, furniture for use and comfort, and if you are fortunate enough to own an heirloom so precious it gives you legitimate cause for worry then for heaven's sake put it away in another room so you can all breathe easily.

Probably you have more sense than to be so obsessive, but particularly if you come home from work to prepare for a midweek dinner party you may despair slightly at the cheerless look of the place and doubt whether anyone could feel comfortable amid the crumby remains of breakfast and the wastepaper of three days' unsorted post and unread news either. The half-hour solution to this problem is relatively simple, though unfortunately rather Superwomanish. First of all, draw the curtains and turn on what you know from experience is the optimum selection of lights; light the fire if it's at all justifiable, and already the place looks attractive. Now, if you have only one reception room, set the table, clearing all old marmalade jars and coffee cups into the kitchen, and papers in one pile on your bed (where they can't get lost or forgotten). Indulge yourself with whole batteries of snowy damask, glittering glassware and vivid napkins if you like, but don't work yourself into a time-consuming frenzy trying to arrange paper napkins as origami waterlilies – they'll only get torn to ribbons by hapless guests attempting to put them to their proper use. A bowl of fruit looks attractive even if it's only full of oranges and lemons clearly not intended for eating, and it's cheaper, quicker and less formal than flower arrangements; a decanter full of wine looks decadently inviting and might even do the wine good, or at least hide the label, and don't forget to check that there is actually some salt and pepper *in* your decorative cruet set now rather than later, though the aim at the moment is to make the place look attractive, not check up on the catering.

There's no need to become hysterical if your table settings don't all match. Only the glossy magazines and Superwoman care about such things; as long as no one item is obtrusively ugly, the overall effect can be enhanced by some variety. An over-matched table can look as intimidating as attractive, the very evenness of everything making it seem an intrusion to do anything so vulgar as eat off it, and you mustn't become so obsessed with your image that you forget about your guests' comfort; besides, you're always going to be stymied by the odd unconsidered extra, like a small pot for the mint sauce or garlic butter, for example, and what will happen when you want to serve three vegetables but have providently provided yourself with two dishes? Odd china can be brought to an art form, with 'harlequin' sets in which no two of the attractive items picked up in junk shops are the same, but this is a sort of reverse Superwomanhood as pernicious in its own way as the other. Nevertheless, sets are not the be-all and end-all of your housewifery – individuality is what we prize in people, after all, so why not reflect it in your possessions? At the very least, you might consider that your passion for uniformity could be laying up countless neuroses for those guests who might want to ask you back but haven't got more than three of anything the same.

Now stand back, and see if the dining part of the room doesn't look hospitable and attractive, and if the cobweb lurking above the picture rail hasn't receded into obscurity. So next turn to the chairs you want people to sit comfortably in, and the tables for their glasses and the bowls of nibbles to stand on. Clear all flat surfaces of yesterday's news, last week's fireside reading and glass-rings – one pile for all papers, again dumped on your bed, and it won't take half a minute – plump up cushions, hoover the clear section of floor if necessary, but don't move any furniture. If you bought flowers, put them in a slightly too narrow vase (so they don't need arranging) in the least interesting corner, and suddenly you have an unfussily neat room in which dust on the mantelpiece or fluff under the chairs won't be visible even to you. This whole operation, including the table setting, really *does* only take half an hour, and it's amazing how much better it makes you feel about the impending ordeal just to have it done.

If you have the luxury of a separate dining room, you may want to reverse the order of operations, but it doesn't make any difference. And the rest of the house, after a quick check to see the bathroom isn't too sordid, and has loo paper and at least one reasonably dry towel in it, can be ignored completely – you will be clearing up the kitchen while you attend to the nibbles and the last-minute things like salad dressing (won't you?) and nobody need see anything else. So now go and change if you're going to; you can perfectly well deal with the rest of the cooking after the guests have arrived, but nothing is guaranteed to make you feel quite so unprepared as being caught in a different persona from the one you intended to present. And the guest who offers to help should be neither surprised nor offended at being given a sharp knife and a cucumber – especially if accompanied by a stiff gin.

Men, if they're around, should always be pressed into service. All too many of them are all too good at kindly promising to deal with the drink, and thinking that's a fair share of the labour. This means he arrives a mere half-hour before the appointed time (by now you've had visions of having to leave your visitors alone and drinkless while you do a mercy dash to the off licence), complaining about the price of booze these days and saying in an injured tone when you greet him with cries of irritated relief 'Well I said I'd do it, didn't I?'. He will then retreat into the sitting room to potter among the bottles, emerging only to upbraid you for running out of ice, ask you where the corkscrew is and 'haven't we got any lemons?' Then he'll be aggrieved when you scream at him.

Even if he can't cook (and can he prove that he can't?) he can peel potatoes, or shop, or wield a vacuum cleaner. A good idea is to make him responsible for at least one complete course – but if he gets out of it lightly by paying a ransom to Parma Ham or Steak Tartare or exotic fruits and cheeses, that's his option, and you mustn't feel put upon by it. You're in the business of reducing your work levels, not increasing his to match; the only circumstances in which his solution is unfair is when you are also bearing the expenses of your own courses separately and he's rolling while you're skint – in this case he must skivvy as well. But a great many men are in any case very good cooks indeed, and enjoy doing it; if yours is one of them just foster his culinary conceit a little and you might find yourself banned from the kitchen completely . . .

Without any help or hindrance from a man, a dinner party can be both more and less of an ordeal. For a start, you won't have had to wrangle and finally compromise on who's coming, when, and what they're going to eat. You will, however, have nobody with whom to share the boring, or simply time-consuming, chores. One way to solve this is to enlist the services of a friend – get him or her to arrive at the same time as you do bringing, say, the pudding under one arm, then you both share the work on the understanding that the favour will be returned. This only works, however, if you know each other extremely well and share the same taste in dinner guests; otherwise neither of you will enjoy yourselves enough to be prepared to repeat the experiment. You will also need to liaise carefully over the menu – it's no good saying 'You do pudding' without mentioning what you're planning to serve before it, or you could end up with the dreaded all cream-based, or all cherry-flavoured, or all beige, meal.

The main mistake the would-be Superwoman makes is to stop at this point, thinking everything's done – forgetting that the evening doesn't stop when the doorbell rings, but starts there. Much more important than the quality of the food and drink or the new-pin neatness of your habitat is, of course, the happiness of your friends and yourself in each other's company. The only way to achieve this is by being relaxed and happy yourself, which means that you can't be tempted to set your guests on edge by showing your nerves, and which also means that you must also immediately forget every rigid rule of etiquette or entertaining that you've ever known. The one rule is that there are no rules. If everyone is contentedly sinking into silliness with their elbows on the table, it is rank folly to insist on moving to 'somewhere more comfortable'; you will ruin everyone's sense of ease by forbidding your helpful friends to carry plates out. Whatever your particular upbringing and fetishes are with regard to table manners, it is incredibly rude to demand that others should follow the same code, so unless a guest is positively offensive (in which case, presumably, you won't have asked him or her anyway, or certainly won't again) everyone should be allowed to do exactly what they feel most comfortable doing. And that, within reason, applies to you too; you can't decide not to fetch the next course at all, but if you want to finish your conversation first, rather than leaping up as the last fork is laid down, you'll probably be doing the rest of them a favour as well. And although your recipes are designed to be foolproof, minor disasters can still happen – if it can't be quickly and quietly rectified, admit it brazenly. I have served an exploded pie unconventionally in the kitchen before, and I've also had to announce that the three-course meal was now a two-course one; in the first case, nobody had the remotest idea that anything had happened, and in the second, they found it so funny, and countered my disaster with so many of their own, that the evening turned from average to superb. Nobody's perfect, and other people's imperfections are endlessly encouraging.

Parties are in many ways much easier than dinners. The level of catering doesn't need to be anything like as high, though the bills will be a lot higher, and a fair amount of the social work can be absorbed by the sheer variety and quantity of guests. The invitation list is simpler to compile, because you don't have to select or match for compatability so exactly, and the numbers are less crucial. On the other hand, you do have to do a lot more sheer physical work, from writing invitations, to carting the provisions back home, to moving furniture, to catering in bulk; and you also need to think a bit further than putting all your friends in one small room with a glass of lukewarm wine in one hand and a sausage on a stick in the other. Superwoman is quite right in her belief that themes make parties work, but she seems also to have all her guests so well-organized that they work as hard for the right effect as she does. You, being less perfect and so more aware of other people's failings, are thoroughly aware too that about thirty per cent of them won't bother to come in character, or whatever you have requested them to come in; won't bring fireworks at all or will bring the same sort; will misread the invitation and expect food where there are only snacks or have eaten when there's a buffet supper. You therefore need to compensate by preparing your background effects more thoroughly. It isn't as arduous as it sounds. I've seen a student party in a garage turned from mediocre to 'original' by covering the walls in newspaper, painting them white, and making everyone sign them in red ink as they arrived (it took three people an afternoon); I've transformed a thirty-foot conventional room into a den of iniquity in less than an hour with four rolls of crepe paper, three red light bulbs and some furniture removing; and I know somebody who added panache to a spring dinner party by holding it to celebrate Michelangelo's birthday. All that was needed, in every case, was just some idea to lift the occasion out of the ordinary.

Food and drink should be incorporated into your theme if you can do it without breaking the bank or leaving everyone hungry (and do make it clear on the invitation what level of catering is going to be on offer). A soup kitchen, for instance, is a more nourishing image of the thirties than are canapés, or a large cold turkey than mince pies of Christmas; you may not be able to afford champagne, but with a little ingenuity you can create startlingly decadent champagne cocktails for the same cost as supplies of red and white plonk. And don't, by the way, forget about drivers and non-drinkers – why should they be palmed off with orange juice or Perrier, when any supermarket can provide a range of much more exciting alternatives: white grape juice, or sparkling apple juice, or one of those delicious citrus cocktails, for example?

Don't fall into the trap, either, of thinking that large numbers make a good party. As with your dinners, so with your larger-scale operations: thirty of the right people will make a much better party than those thirty plus fifteen of the wrong ones. With the right people, the affair will find its own mood and direction, and if you are wise you will follow it, giving only a gentle push if it looks like stagnating. When everyone has just settled down on the floor in animated conversational groups is not the moment to insist on Murder in the Dark; when the dancing area has emptied for the second slow number in succession it's time to give up and play fast ones instead. The purpose of any theme or entertainment provided is to give the initial ice-breaking focus, a refuge from boredom, and perhaps a spirit of curious anticipation; it's not a rigid framework that mustn't be distorted or adapted in any way. Set the image up as completely as you can, and then forget it's there – and you can't lose.

Above all, do try not to be panicked out of making the effort at all. Just as what you really want when you set out to entertain is to see the people you like in a friendly, fun atmosphere, so what they want – you hope – when they accept your invitation is to see you. And even if it does involve a bit of work, though I also hope you've realized it needn't be much, you will probably get asked back – which will save at least one day's worry about the washing up and what can you have for supper. So swallow your false pride, push to the back of your mind your pretensions to perfection, and issue your first invitation for months: you'll be surprised how easy it is.

Children's and business entertaining both fall into slightly different categories from the norm of domestic social life, but by and large the points that arise with the latter are relevant to them as well. Overall, the only lesson to be learned about entertaining is to treat it in the spirit of the word itself: and you're guaranteed to win friends and influence people, and save your nervous system to boot. Sure, you may be out of the competition stakes as far as

Superwoman is concerned, but you and your no doubt ever-growing circle of friends will be a lot more comfortable. And you didn't want to be competing anyway – did you?

# 7

## *A Man's World*

Superwoman wouldn't be complete without a man, and since at thirty-five she is well on her way to the nuclear perfection of 1.8 children and half a dog, he is almost inevitably her husband. He works at something high-pressure, and often either 'creative' or commercially innovative (advertising agencies and small one-man businesses are good places for him) but however tired he is at the end of the day he remains supportive of her role, whether salaried or not, as well. He enjoys cooking when the mood takes him (though there is little evidence that he enjoys washing up afterwards); likes sport of some description, and may be sent off to indulge himself in it on Saturday afternoon, while she prepares for a seductive dîner à deux of steak, chilled white wine, candlelight and a little black dress; on Sundays he fulfils his role as a family man with some DIY, a drink together at the local (children permitting) and the ceremonial carving of the roast. They have a satisfactory sex life which takes full account of the female orgasm, positions other than missionary and leaving the lights on. Despite the fact that he gives some help in the house and is proud of her career, she never demands any real domestic equality of him; Superwoman knows, after all, how competent she is, and knows too that men are like children really – if she were run over by a bus tomorrow he'd be absolutely *helpless*. They discuss their relationship calmly and openly, and understand each other's point of view rather than having screaming rows: all in all they get along very contentedly.

Superwoman's best friend is a couple of years older than her and divorced, with two children from her disastrously early marriage. Her ex-husband treated her appallingly, but luckily liberation came along and gave her the impetus to divorce him: now she leads an independent life in the formerly marital home and vows she will never let herself get tied to a man again. Her lovers come and go, but she never lets them move in; they get on marvellously with the children (who nevertheless really respect them when male authority is occasionally called for) and shower her with gifts and weekends in Paris, at which times she dumps her children on Superwoman, packs her Janet Reger and disappears at the drop of a plane ticket. Superwoman admires her enormously, regarding her with a mixture of awe and envy – in her heart she knows that she couldn't ever really be happy with that sort of life, but it is so encouraging that there are women who can: and so she lives out her *Scruples*-style fantasies through her friend over endless glasses of wine at the kitchen table, and lies loyally to the ex-husband or out-of-favour lovers when necessary on her behalf. She gains a vicarious feeling of outrageousness herself from the relationship, and is able to feel recklessly sophisticated by association, as well as playing her favourite housemother role in times of crisis: she understand the problems of today's women, but copes with them herself without having become strident.

She feels an occasional twinge of envy, too, for her little sister: Heaven knows she never had a moment's doubt when Geoff came along, but there are times when she looks back wistfully at the fun she used to have before adult life began in earnest. Young Sarah seems to have the best of all possible worlds. She says she's going to marry and have children, but not for four or five years yet, and in the meanwhile she's got a fantastic job – she didn't have to battle for it the way Superwoman did, either – and seems to spend almost every night with a different man in the most carefree way imaginable: and of course, without the responsibility of a 'proper' home she's free to indulge herself in all sorts of new outfits, exotic holidays, and generally exciting behaviour. But she *is* nearly twenty-five, so she'd better be careful she doesn't miss the husband boat . . .

One way and another, Superwoman is pretty well obsessed by men, and despite the wide-ranging, multiple-choice nature of the features on man-related topics that rate so much paper and ink in her favourite newspapers and magazines – from herpes to housework-sharing via everything in between – she is also quite definite that they're designed as eventual husband material. She is simply exploring a lot more angles to make as sure as possible that her intended mate will be the right one: because there is never a moment's doubt, however peripherally men appear in any piece, of the underlying assumption that you've either got one, or you're looking. The *Cosmopolitan* feature with the rallying headline 'Cheers, You're Single!', for example, goes on, after detailing the advantages of your untrammelled existence, to an extraordinary piece of double-think by offering a 'good-man guide: whom you'll find, where and when' – presumably to help you trammel yourself as rapidly as possible. As if that weren't enough, it underlines Superwoman's philosophy even more heavily in an 'Ode to Single' with the plea 'I wonder if it has occurred/That married life can be deferred . . . Do people know that girls like me/Can wait to have a family?' (Marcelle d'Argy Smith, *Cosmopolitan* January 1984). See? Single is great – but only temporarily. *Over 21*, in its March 1984 issue, gives straight-from-the-shoulder warnings about 'The Hopes, Happiness and Hang-Ups of Marriage' – not to be seen as a universal panacea, not always the right answer, and so on – but they include in the same issue a more than usually simplistic guide to choosing the perfect partner by his star sign. The clear assumption behind *Company*'s feature on the self-delusions of mistresses (March 1984) is that you really want him for your husband, while the piece on role models in the same issue announces unequivocally that women want both a career and a family . . .

They're all doing it all the time. They'd probably all be

horrified, defensive and indignant if it were pointed out to them what they were doing, though they might claim that 'That's what the readers believe' – in which case they'd be absolutely right. Not only Superwoman, but the rest of us confused followers, know somewhere deep in the bottom of our hearts that to attract the love of a good man is the ultimate female sucsex symbol, and anything else is sheer compensation: this is particularly true now the sexual revolution has left us free *not* to marry, paradoxically, because it's also left men free not to 'have' to marry us either. You may mock Superwoman's unquestioning domesticity; you may relish your career and your freedom; you may insist that there could be no compensation for having to share your precious personal living space; you may demand total commitment to the housework before you'll so much as have a drink with him – but somehow, without a man, you're still waiting for the curtain to go up on your *real* life. With one, you're waiting for the grand finale of the white wedding, so you can close that production and start living happily ever after; once you're married, you're ticking over until the romance happens somewhere in between the strain of the wedding and the onset of companionship. There is some corner of a woman's mind that is forever waiting for a knight on a white charger to take over and ride roughshod over the rest of it.

There is almost certainly nothing you can do about this faint revisionist yearning, except to tell yourself it's a fantasy and life isn't like that, which you're probably already doing. This is unfortunate, since it sits uneasily with the rest of your modern philosophy of life, counting on you to conform to an image that doesn't fit. The equal partnership you know is your right doesn't offer much room for a full suit of knightly armour; a white charger is a decided liability to a practical mind; you are very unlikely to be able to envisage yourself behaving like one of those wet, idiotic damsels in distress; your radical sisters – and you at least partly agree with them – would disapprove strongly of your drowning in anyone's eyes, especially a chauvinist chevalier's; you have a deep conviction that when the dragon appears you'll deal with it a great deal more competently than your make. And the fundamental problem, when you're working on the casting for this idyll, is that not many men ever wanted to be knights on white chargers in the first place – and now they're allowed to say they won't play.

You may be unsure as yet of exactly how, as a would-be Superwoman, you're supposed to relate to a man, but he has even less idea of how he's meant to behave towards you. The confusing and contradictory reams of advice and instruction your mentors pour out may quarrel with your earlier conditioning and with itself, but it is there, and it's all positive – whatever particular line you're being encouraged to take is offering you an improvement on your previous position. For men, however, the changes are not only uncodified, but they're almost all negative: at every encounter women gain ground and men lose it, and there doesn't seem to be a solid defensible line behind which they can regroup. Their only real gain is itself a negative one – the freedom to abandon their *machismo*, admit that they don't like football or want to win the Rat Race, do like cooking and enjoy talking to women rather than picking them up, is an ability to give up doing something, not an opportunity to do something new. While any man might be glad to be liberated from his muscle-bound image and allowed to relax, he has no indication of what image he's supposed to adopt instead, and it's hard to see why anyone would enjoy the sensation of having the ground moved from under his feet, in however good a cause. So there is an understandable, panicky confusion in the ranks, and far from remaining in their old formation, which the oncoming regiment of women still seem to see before them, a defeated army of men is scattering to a variety of new positions without even the benefit of orders from headquarters.

In the hills, the resistance continue to snipe away from their more and more isolated strongholds, taking refuge in macho extremism. These include the old-school-men (which doesn't necessarily mean old) who proclaim vigorously that women are wonderful, bless 'em, just as they are, but a chap still needs a bit of a rest from them somewhere; or they'll never be able to work an oil rig, so why can't they calm down and accept what they *are* good at? Semi-old- school types announce defiantly that they were brought up to be polite to ladies, and they can't stop opening doors and walking on the outsides of pavements now; these may be the same men who will embark on risqué jokes after a couple of drinks, and then virtuously declare 'No, another time, not suitable for mixed company', leering at you, just before the punchline (and in my experience, you probably knew the joke anyway, and hadn't found it funny the first time). Or they will greet some innocuous remark from you with a mock-terrified 'I say, got to watch our step, we've got a libber here!'. The young macho male either models himself on a rock star, and persists in believing – or says he believes – that your demands for equality simply mean you're dying to leap into bed with him: if you think it's worth trying to separate his talk from his pillow, he'll grandly grant you the right to do whatever you like – as long as it doesn't interfere with his dinner. Alternatively, he simply fails to understand what all the fuss is about, and continues to treat you like a cross between his nanny and an inflatable doll, sublimely unaware that there's anything wrong with this approach, because sublimely confident that women really like a man to be masterful. Don't worry, if your heart has filled with horror: these groups can be largely ignored. Gradually they will realize that their support is petering out fast, and the sniping is already becoming a mere nuisance for the sake of form rather than any serious attempt at victory.

Other men have gone to the opposite extreme by establishing themselves quickly as trusted collaborators, and infiltrating the senior posts in the information departments. Uncle Tom Crabtree and all are more zealous in their condemnation and exposure of men than the most violently matriarchal of women, and like all collaborators they are viewed with a certain amount of distrust on both sides. If he *really* likes women more than men, why didn't he say so fifteen years ago – he was a columnist already then? Why, if he cares so passionately about women's rights, did he have to wait for them to be brought so forcibly to his attention before he acted?

Along with the collaborators come the zealots: those men who, you get the feeling, do genuinely believe in the justice of the cause, but who you also can't help feeling make both it and themselves slightly ridiculous through an excess of fervour from the wrong direction, as if Henry Ford were vigorously denouncing traffic pollution. They are followed by the court jesters: 'token men', who are given positions in the women's media in order to write amusing articles about the battle of the sexes from the losing side, in which the men always end up looking absurd. Some of these, to their credit, are slowly turning into fifth columnists, and using their articles to point out that men are a confused and beaten enemy who need some help and understanding in order to rehabilitate themselves: the time has come for magnanimity in victory, and this sort of inflammatory suggestion is now not only tolerated, but gaining currency.

But these are all minority splinter-groups: by far the largest bulk of the male army has, as an occupied nation must, either integrated itself or taken cover. For the man who integrates, life is fraught with peril and uncertainty. He sees clearly that the cause was just and the ground has been rightly won; that he has in fact got away with better than he deserves so far, and that he must now atone for the sins of his fathers by avoiding them scrupulously himself. Consequently, he walks in perpetual fear that he might unwittingly be committing some sexist solecism of such terrible magnitude as to condemn himself accidentally forever. Small crises occur every day: is he allowed to buy her a drink, or admire her hair? If he offers his seat to a pregnant woman will she accept it or belabour him with her umbrella? Must he give up drinking beer and watching Match of the Day? Should he cumbersomely write 'he or she' wherever the third person singular appears in his twenty-page report? Ought he to address her as Ms (and how do you pronounce it)? Does his favourite flying jacket proclaim an offensively macho subconscious? And he is always uneasily aware that even if he avoids all these terrible traps and more he is in the wrong already, just by being born and brought up in that country of the pre-feminist era – so he can't win anyway.

It's a lot easier if he takes cover – and the men who do so are actually being extremely helpful in reinforcing the Superwoman Trap. Their trick is to admit, freely and frankly, that women can do just about everything as well as or better than them, and that they know they're intolerably self-centred and deserve to be horsewhipped for it – and then to sit back in unrepentant contentment and let Superwoman get on with it. It may involve him in the occasional nuisance of obligingly wielding a wooden spoon or vacuum – though for the talented, it's easy enough to make such a mess with either that it will be quickly seized from his limp grasp – but it saves him from any further exertion in almost any other direction. Superwoman is only too eager to prove that she can work three times as hard and beat him in the Rat Race, while running the home like clockwork, changing car tyres with the best of them, organizing the baby like Mussolini did the trains, filling in his tax returns as well as her own, knowing the news headlines, paying for her round and generally behaving like a superior nanny in every possible way. If he has prepared the way properly, a bunch of flowers and a penitent 'I told you I was a selfish brute' will usually count as sufficient recompense for most lapses, and before either of them knows it he'll have got away without having had to change his spots at all. A lot of colonies used to exist very happily in this position for a very long time, and so, indeed, did a lot of women under the tutelage of men: it might be disturbing to draw the parallel too closely in view of the end result in both cases, but for the moment the situation is both convenient and comfortable for the man in question. All the more so because nobody, least of all himself, will ever question the purity of his motives.

Inevitably the man or men you are actually trying to deal with will be a mixture of some or all of these types, probably with the last one prevailing. And as though that weren't confusing enough already, your different relationship with him will give rise to different reactions and problem areas. So although there is no doubt that you need to understand what's making him behave like that (and perhaps even sympathize a little), you'll have quite enough to do sorting out your own attitudes without worrying too much about his at the moment: they, like so many other things, can't be straightened out in this generation anyway.

If you're a properly brought up would-be Superwoman, you will feel called upon from time to time to take exception to countless sexist offences, from whatever type of man: but you will also be unsure about how relevant or important they are, and in extreme cases whether in fact you oughtn't, in one of your other roles such as Superworkingwoman, be adopting them instead of protesting at them. Once again, you are the only person who can really answer that. You might only find smutty jokes offensive if they're not funny as well – but have friends who would happily pillory the teller and others who feel they must tell them themselves to show they belong; you might object to being 'put down' as a woman and insist on changing your own tyres and carrying your own suitcase, but flirt wantonly in pursuit of your own ends: the contradictions are there within you just as much as they are in him. Gradually a sensible compromise level of acceptability will be reached; in the meanwhile all you can do is shake up your principles with your common sense and see what comes out. And you might also do the offending man the favour of explaining why, rather than just snarling 'Sexist!' If you don't tell him, how will he ever learn?

Whatever your relationship, whether you're married, living together, manless or surrounded by lovers too numerous to mention, you are going through the same transitional difficulties in rearranging your social dealings with men. Womanhood is no longer a simple, cut-and-dried matter of the race to find a good husband, so that while he's out at work or in his club, or when you're shutting your eyes and thinking of England, at least you'll be doing so in comfortable surroundings and not being actively ill-treated: or, alternatively, carving out a much tougher life for yourself as a fallen woman; which could be a lot more fun if you made a financial success of it, a disaster if you didn't.

Nowadays the dividing lines have all been split and broken, yet we've not only not managed to rid ourselves of the conviction that marriage is the final refuge of the respectable, but we've actually raised our demands of it so high that in this area at least her followers are bidding to overtake Superwoman. Not only must 'he' be a good husband in the old-fashioned sense, combining the virtues of success with those of kindness, and being acceptable, preferably, to our parents and friends, but he must also have accepted totally the march of equality, and the consequent importance of your needs, desires and priorities as well as his own; he must be a sensitive and stimulating lover as well; but above all he must be, not just *a* husband, but the absolutely, only right husband or no husband at all. Which is a highly laudable aim, but one rather hard to come to terms with when the alternative to the 'right' husband is not the nearly right husband, but continuing single until the right one arrives, if ever – single being a state that neither you nor your contemporaries really regard yet as anything other than a slight misfortune. Similarly, if you're going to spurn the dreary domesticities of matrimony in favour of a spicier life, you can't just settle for being happily depraved: you've got to set yourself up as a cross between Madame de Pompadour and Joan Collins, with a strong strain of Olga Korbut's gymnastic talent and Germaine Greer's pre-1984 philosophy thrown in. And if you're single and manless, you have to be pretty brave to be caught spending the evening in on your own watching a soap opera, when you could be out there learning German for Computers or discoing the night away amid the easy camaraderie of the young, fun set . . . In other, words, just because you've been allowed to choose, you now have to work extremely hard at proving that you're happy with your choice, instead of just being it.

Moreover, though the rules for men may be uncertain at the moment, any man still has very much the upper hand when it comes to the expectations of a relationship. Whereas he mustn't behave as if he were footloose and fancy-free any more, devoting himself to wine, women, song and the rugby club, and he must make some effort to help around the house and appreciate both what you do for him and what you are yourself, the implication is still that unless he behaves like a completely insensitive boor and cad you'll have no cause for complaint. You, on the other hand, as you are constantly being warned, must work non-stop to 'keep' him: but he can be expected to walk out on you just because he's bored – and, what's more, it'll be your fault if he is.

If you're a would-be Superwoman with a husband or permanent man, you will know that you should be worrying about familiarity breeding contempt, and keeping yourself attractive rather than sliding into a rut. There are women even now whose husbands have never seen them without make-up, or with dirty hair, and who flirt religiously with them at least once a week, but even without going to that sort of extreme you can work up a pretty good head of guilt and over-anxiety about your scruffy weekend jeans or broken fingernails, or the fact that you've been too engrossed in your book, or too tired from your heavy day at the office, to listen to his problems all evening. And you are supposed also to be putting your own motives under constant mental review, to make sure that you aren't compromising your ideals in any way; that he is worthy of your new female status, and that you are completely, passionately in love without a moment's remission for good behaviour. And if you're living together in unmarried bliss, there is the added niggling concern that he doesn't love you enough to marry you, and you're settling for less than you should: instantly countered, of course, by the brisk self-reassurance that your relationship doesn't need to be bolstered by artificial aids, that marriage isn't necessary for your happiness – so that now you can also worry about what's wrong with you to make you hold obstinately to such old-fashioned views . . .

You will also be concerned with the practicalities of communal life, and with your deep conviction that you aren't looking after him properly. You get frustrated if he doesn't take a genuinely equal load of the chores – will go shopping, but only if you give him a list; cook, but keep asking you 'where you keep the pepper' (*you* keep it, please note: it's nothing to do with him); decorate, but with you constantly on hand as builder's mate; change nappies, but returns 'your' child like a hot potato if it cries for longer than half a minute. One of the most infuriating things is man's willingness to 'help' – because it is totally impossible, in my experience anyway, to make him understand that 'helping' implies you're doing something extra that isn't normally your job, and the very use of the word underlines a mistaken belief in his role in an equal partnership. The other cause for frustrated fury is the injured cry 'But if only you'd *told* me we'd run out of loo paper/the carpet was filthy/you wanted me to wash up . . .' : why should he need you to *tell* him, when he's got just as many eyes and the same equipment for thinking with as you have?

On the other hand, if you don't wait on him hand and foot (and particularly if you've attached yourself to the sort of person I have, who thinks the place is a tip when I'm just congratulating myself on it being moderately tidy, and who therefore does infinitely more housework than I ever do) that old Superwoman magic can work on you until you're a nervous wreck. You can torture yourself daily with little stabs of guilt, castigate yourself for your idleness, uselessness and general inefficiency, for being such an unnatural woman, and finally convince yourself that you have nothing to offer him he could possibly want. It's only too easy to believe that you have failed him – or, more unnerving still, will fail to keep him – if you don't at least provide him with a daily laundry and restaurant service: after all, you're exposed to enough propaganda telling you it is so. The logical result of this reaction, of course, is that you'll drive both of you demented by turning the housework into a god that must be served at all costs, never have time for anything else at all, and finally lose him anyway, mentally if not geographically, be treating him as something to dust round, clean up after, and stoke up at regular intervals – but who's thinking logically when ridden with guilt?

The urge towards a permanent relationship, preferably marriage, is actually on the increase at the moment, and the vast majority of women in a recent survey accepted that they would bear the brunt of the cooking and cleaning, even after a full day's work. 'Conceding to such a stereotype superwoman image may create resentment and anger for women, but repudiating it can lead to unmanageable feelings of guilt and inadequacy' points out Nigella Lawson (*Observer*, 26 February 1984), and although we've come a long way from the time when Shirley Conran could believe that 'A husband who doesn't mind the occasional snack meal in a crisis – or even cooks it – is worth his weight in platinum' (*Superwoman*) Ms Lawson is right to recognize that we still can't fully dissociate our emotional commitment from our traditional caring role. Moreover, since all the imperatives of our new role are geared to us proving that we *can* do it all, and do it better, even if we shouldn't necessarily, the trap here becomes distinctly two-pronged.

The only way out of the 'housework is love' syndrome is to insist loudly to yourself, your man, and anyone else who'll listen that you are appallingly sluttish, a useless cook, and anyway firmly believe that until he has been forced into doing more than his share he'll never accept an equal division. If you say it often enough, at least the people you say it to will begin to accept that you might mean it, even if *you* don't, and eventually it could even become more or less true. It won't stop you feeling guilty at heart – but you'll get a lot better at pretending you don't.

As for the business of 'keeping him interested' – I wouldn't be at all surprised if one of the main subconscious urges towards marriage weren't a strong desire to relax your eternal, on-your-toes vigilance, so competitively vital in an open-ended relationship where there are no safety chains to hinder him from slipping away through the first yawn. And yet I find it difficult to believe that even such poor creatures as men are supposed to be can really be that easily bamboozled by a new hairstyle or a different colour eyeshadow, so simply seduced by a steamed pudding, or enthralled forever by your sparkling opinions on the latest television serial. What's more, when he married or moved in with you he presumably had some idea of what he was letting himself in for – turning yourself into a different person, whether housekeeper or harlot, seems an illogical way to maintain the initial attraction. And surely he will be more interested in you as a person if you are interesting in yourself than if you engulf your own personality in a neurotic, cramping obsession with his? The partnerships I know that work best operate on the basis of common ground between two individuals, not on fusion – though inevitably there are limits to the desirable level of separateness, which will be different for everyone. If you still think you're letting him down, think back to what we discussed earlier, about the assumption that only the female has to work at keeping interest alive – and by the time you've got properly indignant about that you shouldn't have any room left for guilt at all.

Ultimately, if you can examine your character objectively, and honestly decide whether *you* like it, or whether you are prepared to accept certain traits in the overall context of the rest, then this should be the only criterion on which you base any attempt to change yourself – not what you think he thinks you should be, like a game of consequences. You might very easily be wrong about what you think he thinks, and besides, you would be foolish to seek his approval at the expense of your own – it's very difficult for anybody to like someone who doesn't like him – or herself. It might seem equally difficult at first to persuade your man to accept a reduction in his expectations of you, but it is rarely impossible: not least because your'take me or leave me' attitude leaves him free to demand a similar liberality from you with regard to himself – usually in all sorts of completely inappropriate circumstances, but at least the ensuing rows should keep your wits lively. And should it happen that you end up having to admit to total incompatability on a fundamental issue or characteristic, then you're almost certainly in the wrong relationship; but if you've applied the criterion of self-liking honestly you will be left, after you've waved him goodbye, with somebody you don't mind living with.

If you are single, you will have a different set of problems. Firstly, and most difficult, you have to convince yourself that being single doesn't mean you're inadequate, without going to the opposite extreme and convincing everyone else that you think you're too good for them. It's a tricky equation, because the latter is so often a very natural defensive reaction to the first belief, which as we've already seen remains obstinately prevalent. There may be nothing you can effectively do to banish the vision of your knight on his white charger completely, but you can concentrate on the positive aspects of your freedom. Not, in the way the articles, singles holidays tour operators and in-depth television teams do, on the silly trivia of not having to share the toothpaste, or being free to pick up a partner, but rather on the freedom to develop yourself the way you want to, spared from the terrible traps to which your man-committed sisters are doomed. It is extraordinarily hard to persuade yourself that you don't have to grab at every trousered straw that floats your way or risk drowning; equally, of course, an over-eager grab on your part can send him scuttling away in terror anyway, so you can very quickly drive yourself into a vicious circle with that game.

Alternatively you might be, like Superwoman's best friend, gracious hostess to a whole court of suitors – in which case you certainly look from the outside as if you've got your options worked out very well indeed. But again you could actually be a victim of your own propaganda, persuaded that it is not only your right but your duty to indulge your sexual equality for the sake of those who will follow – and without any thought to the possibility that your mind may not be ready to assimilate the same freedoms that your body is more than capable of. Or you might have established your existence firmly on the physical plane in order to prevent yourself from being emotionally hurt (I know a number of women who have done so, none of them happy); this doesn't seem to me to be a terribly good idea either, since you almost certainly *are* going to get hurt – in which case, it's a bit wasteful not to have jumped in feet first and enjoyed yourself beforehand.

Both of you will have a fair amount of trouble in convincing some men – those who are even more hidebound by their view of the traditional sex roles than you are – that when you say 'no' to them 'no' is exactly what you mean. I don't mean the partisans, particularly: more insidious is the faithful sheepdog who remains smugly convinced that if he just stays around long enough you'll see reason in the end, because it is a truth universally acknowledged that you must be in search of a husband to settle down with, and he is obviously as well qualified for the role as the next man. Short of proclaiming lesbianism or madness in the family, there isn't a lot you can do, because no amount of clear, kind explanation that you just don't love him will ever penetrate his armour. And you will run into quite as many problems explaining that when you say 'yes' you mean that too: a lot of men tend to be intimidated by independent women (and indeed may only have been asking because they expected a negative answer, which is bad luck on one or both of you if you do want to accept) and you yourself may well have spent so long fostering your image as unattainable that nobody will easily believe your volte-face. And you must also remember, of course, as if the media would let you forget, that where a wife or permanent girlfriend must be constantly on her guard against being boring, so a single girl must be ever vigilant against threatening his freedom with the suggestion that she might wish to extend their relationship, and a mistress depends for her continuing success on never having an off day and always being available when he calls.

But whatever the social background to your problems, they all come down in the end to your choices and decisions over whether, with whom and how closely you want to become involved: and if you cling firmly to your self-image, and treat the self-liking principle as your life-line in a choppy sea of conflicting ideologies, desires and social conditioning, then you can't come to much harm.

There is one other category of relationship which rarely gets mentioned at all in the volumes written about the interactions of men and women: that of straightforward friendship. Friendship doesn't generally get much of a press in any case, or if it does it's on the basis of your friends of the same sex bolstering you up in moments of sexual trauma; yet friendship is just as important as any sexual relationship, if not more so. And friendships between men and women are almost completely ignored, because we don't know the rules for them: both sexes still suspect the other of having designs on their virtue (and in the women's magazines the pronoun 'he' still carries the strong presumption that 'he' is husband fodder); as if this conditioning didn't provide sufficient hindrance to easy camaraderie between the sexes, then the new and vexed question of sexism offers plenty more. It's difficult to feel enough at your ease for a genuine friendship to develop if you're guarding your tongue the entire time.

Which is a pity, because cross-sexual friendships can be tremendously rewarding, and if women can learn to treat men as friends rather than as ravaging animals it can only help them to behave that way. Men, in fact, are probably much readier either to offer or to accept friendship than you are; they are also admittedly less likely to find their innocent treatment of the oposite sex as part of the human race being embarrassingly misinterpreted. But we do as much to foster these misinterpretations as men do themselves: confusion about our sexual roles is by no means a prerogative of the male sex, and women too inhibited by the possibility of being misunderstood to attempt friendship with men at all do nothing to clarify the situation. Yet if you do make a habit of treating men as equal human beings, you stand a pretty good chance of being pleasantly surprised by being treated as a human being in return.

I haven't said anything about love with a capital 'L', because only you know about that and how it works for you: there is absolutely no advice less general and still valid that anyone else can give you about your own emotions. Eager advice-givers have always seemed to me to be slightly suspect, for even if they were in full possession of the facts, characters and circumstances concerned in any problem (which no agony auntie and very few friends are) their advice will almost inevitably take a black-and-white view based on principle rather than practice. When they raise their arms in horror at your account of his glass-throwing binge last night and announce firmly that of course you must leave him, they are speaking in happy ignorance of the complex code of acceptability and unacceptability that you have worked out for yourselves – and you no doubt modestly forebore to mention your own prowess in the plate-throwing stakes too. Similarly the helpful friend who undertakes to advise you on how to win or keep your man forgets that you are not her and don't necessarily work on the same assumptions (or indeed, given the usual quality of such unsolicited advice, that men might not be as gullible as she thinks). Certainly, friendly post-mortems can be useful in pointing out the inconsistencies, intolerances, and pure idiocies in your behaviour, but that is as far as their usefulness extends, and after you've listened you're on your own. I suppose you might consider this a bleak or even cynical doctrine, but I find it rather a comforting assertion of self-determination – a relief, in fact, that when it comes down to the really important decisions I can ignore all those contradictory gurus and use my own common sense.

It's impossible to talk about men and women without sex getting in on the act – everywhere! The major social, physical and psychological obsession of the past two decades can hardly be thought to have avoided leaving its impression on Superwoman: an impression, though, that can be more than a little blurred. You already know, because your mother and Superwoman and Mills & Boon all told you, that it's the culmination of a total spiritual union and its physical aspects can therefore be loftily ignored. You also know, because the sixties and the first feminists told you, that it is a purely physical pleasure and you should ignore any other view of it as a residual emotional hang-up. Naturally you are too sensible to believe, as the new puritans seem to think you do, that you are duty bound to leap into bed with every chance acquaintance just because society has decreed that you may; but conversely you might well believe that you're suffering from a severe psychological disturbance and social retardation if you tend towards monogamy. The best rationalization of these initial contradictions that you're likely to come up with is that obviously there's sex and sex, and it all depends on the circumstances, which is banal but true; or that it's all a matter of female conditioning, which will change immediately we achieve true equality with men, which sounds better, but isn't.

Actually it won't change, because a good deal of the fantastic talk about man's freewheeling sex life is just that – talk and fantasy. Remember, if your early training was in protecting yourself scrupulously from male advances, his was in usually frustrated pursuit of the elusive mystery you were protecting: mentally, until the sexual revolution blasted the whole charade wide open, you were each as likely as the other to be ignorant, inexperienced and generally confused. It is certainly true that the physical act of sex has been historically less weighted with consequence for him than for you and can therefore be more easily separated from his emotional life and approached more irresponsibly (or without hang-ups, depending on which philosophical vocabulary you choose), but it would be maligning him to assume that he never brought any emotional commitment into the bedroom at all. Nor is the monogamous man a unique or even particularly rare species; simply one adept at cryptic colouration in order to blend better with a male society committed to a macho self-image – which may be moral cowardice of a sort, but no more so than your own when you hid your pills from your mother, or silently allowed your friends to believe that you'd 'gone all the way' with Alan at the school dance.

Like it or not, sex has always been a highly competitive sport – but until recently the competition was reserved for locker-room boasting or giggling confidences with the girls. Now, when every newspaper, magazine, radio and TV programme and probably school curriculum has 'come out' and discussed your sexual options and rights freely in full frontal, it's no longer good enough to preserve a knowing silence when the conversation turns – as it will – to your comparative sex lives. When you either 'did it' or didn't, that was easy; but today you have to discuss your preferences in the various ways of 'doing it', as well as asserting your absolute right to the multiple orgasm, the dominant role, clitoral stimulation and the full scope of the Kama Sutra: the competition has necessarily been extended to between the sheets as well as behind the bike sheds.

With the spirit of sex as an athletic contest comes automatically the depressingly clinical tone of a training manual, a therapeutic atmosphere to the diagnosis of desire, which encourages an earnest joylessness in the pursuit of what's supposed to be, *pace* the sexual revolution, 'Fun, fun, fun!' Far from relieving us of our inhibitions, as it claimed it would, this public-confession a itemization of the paths to pleasure has only created a whole lot more, and it's easy to lose sight of the purpose of instruction when you get bogged down in the step-by-step, like learning irregular verbs with no inkling that eventually they'll turn into French. And woman's society is obsessed by the individual steps: the shame of failing to achieve multiple orgasm (never mind if you were having a pretty good time without any, or your single ones rival Krakatoa – it's quantity, not quality, that counts); the certainty that something's wrong with you if you aren't turned on by clitoral stimulation; the guilt of falling below the national average of 2.4 sexual encounters an hour; the panic terror of impotence or frigidity if all one of you wants to do after a harrassing day is to go to sleep; the embarrassment of admitting that you find position 473 hideously uncomfortable; the damage to your psyche if you can't turn on sex like a tap with anyone, anywhere . . .

But if women are feverishly training for fitness to enter the sexual games, at least they have got a comprehensive programme to follow from scratch: spare a thought for the men, who have got to unlearn an awful lot of their athletic style before they can be allowed to compete in the same event. This is not surprisingly a tremendous shock to the male system. He's been used to sailing into his standard routine in the certainty of straight sixes every time: now the rules and the steps are all different, and he's not at all sure what he has to do to get even 5.5s. Then to crown it all, you're allowed to stop him and make corrections in mid-performance, and positively encouraged at the end calmly to tell the poor panting sod that he rated 4.7, not a bad effort, but he should pay a bit more attention to the following moves . . . It's enough to put anyone off for life.

All is not bleak point-scoring any more, however. We have come to a new era of sexual maturity, in which sheer animal (ie physical) gratification does not satisfy our ever-hungry minds: you now have to consider whether you are 'ready for the *new* love', which has recently been discovered in America. Basically, 'the *new* love' consists of the peak of physical perfection you can achieve 'together' with regular work-outs according to the athletic rules as before, allied to and enhanced by a deeply sensitive emotional awareness of each other (as in the old love): the whole leading to a total sensual and spiritual bliss, or alternatively a complete breakdown of relations before you get there. In the latter case, you could try 'the *new* celibacy' – it only means you don't have to have sex unless you want to, which by now I shouldn't think either of you do, quite possibly ever. In other words, the glossy magazines have worked out that they may have gone a bit too far, and are now back-pedalling furiously (though they'll still never catch up with Germaine Greer).

Needless to say, they had gone too far, and much of the so-called helpful advice they've been churning out is dangerous lunacy. (And I don't suppose I'm alone in the irreverent and almost irresisitible temptation to try a complete set of manoeuvres with a stopwatch to see what the result would be – I suspect a hilarious fiasco.) But although men and women will no doubt continue happily to do the oddest things with and to each other for the oddest reasons, and will still refrain by and large from gratuitous criticism, the damage is already done. Not because you are actually going through the score card on a meticulous points system, or even probably in most circumstances voice any opinion at all beyond the tried and tested 'Thank you, darling, that was wonderful' (which will continue to be uttered, nine times out of ten, after as many a 1.4 performance as a 5.9) – but because the unspoken niggle of dissatisfaction is implanted uneasily in the back of your mind, telling you that you haven't really got it right yet.

This anxiety does apply to men as well as women, but for many a man the fact that his own sexual satisfaction is comparatively simple to achieve (and his consequent real difficulty in therefore understanding the complexity of yours) acts as a powerfully reassuring anaesthetic. Moreover, the physical instruction manuals have very little to promise him beyond the prospect of an increase in an already highly pleasurable sensation. You, however, are assumed to have been deriving little or no enjoyment at all from sex before they were there to teach you how, and now you're being offered – if not forcibly saddled with – the moon as your goal: a goal that, like all Superwoman's goals, is set at an impossibly high standard. And of course, in true Superwoman style, you are being sold the promise of emotional fulfilment as the reward of practical application: work hard and be efficient, and happiness will result.

The trouble with this maxim is that it works even less well with sex than with most other areas of your endeavour, since Superwoman's all work and no play philosophy is not really conducive to the relaxation required for most enjoyable sexual sensations, physical or emotional. What's more, it's a philosophy based in this case on a false premise, for the work is going into the success of the play, a paradox that Superwoman doesn't seem entirely to have grasped either. The only people for whom sex is pure work are presumably those who get paid for it, and these can also be the only ones for whom there is an absolute standard of right or wrong, good or bad, in the exercise. You know perfectly well at heart that all that matters is that you should – preferably both – be enjoying yourself: all you need to do is to banish from your mind the ridiculous idea that it's possible for you to be enjoying yourself in the wrong way. You could also bear in mind that, as Woody Allen and some enlightened writers have already tried to point out, sex is essentially pretty well the funniest human occupation ever invented: perhaps the solemn quest for the perfect orgasm will turn out one day to have made a real contribution to our sex lives simply by virtue of being so laughable . . .

In bed or out of it, man and Superwoman isn't going to stop being an awkward liaison for a while yet, but it needn't continue to be such a dreadful one. It would be facile to suggest you 'just act normal' in the best tradition of the television crook or the Briton faced with the unusual when neither you nor he has a very firm idea of what *is* normal – but you could make a determined effort to stop analysing all vestiges of normality out of existence, do what your natural inclinations suggest, and regret it afterwards. Because although there's always bound to be some cause for regret, major or minor, it would be much more regrettable not to have had a hell of a good time to show for it.

# 8

# *Our Bodies Ourselves*

It is not enough for Superwoman simply to be fulfilled and successful: she must also look it. The obsession with doing so fills almost as many pages of her magazines, marginally more of her newspapers, and certainly more shelves in her local bookshop than her obsession with men – since, of course, looking the part is a vital step towards becoming it, a man is vital to her fulfilment and success, and she won't get or keep one without the looks.

So Superwoman has a body beautiful. She has a model figure already, naturally, which means she is over 5′8″ and usually slim, though she can get away with being big-bosomed or hippy if she's really tall, and with being less than 5′6″ if she's sylph-like. Her skin is carefully tended and monitored under the discreetly effective make-up to ensure that it keeps its youthful bloom; her hair is neatly groomed and burnished to a healthy gloss; her fingernails are perfectly trimmed and varnished and her legs always newly waxed. At work she wears a lot of pencil-line suits in navy, grey and beige, but lightens the severity of their surrogate-male lines with careful casual touches such as bright scarves, softly tied shirts, lace collars or jokey bow ties; at home she favours Jaeger, Country Casuals, Liberty prints and Laura Ashley as well as the ubiquitous designer jeans and vivid fuchsia flying suits. None of her clothes are ever missing a button or trailing a thread from the hem, nor less than perfectly pressed, and she never snags her tights or scuffs her shoes either: she looks consistently well-dressed, but rarely startling unless she's in full evening rig. She slims at the hint of a hamburger, and knows all the trendy diets off by heart, from Scarsdale to F-plan to Beverley Hills via the by-ways of momentarily popular fads like bananas, or high-carbohydrate, or steak and white wine; for weeks on end she will comb supermarkets and slave away in the kitchen to meet their exacting requirements with religious dedication to the cause of four pounds' weight loss a week.

When Superwoman first emerged, this regime would have been enough for her: now, however, she has to aim for beauty through inner health as well. Only tip-top physical condition is good enough, and it's got to be achieved 'naturally'. Lotte Berk, Jane Fonda, aerobic classes and dance studios called after all sorts of exotic fruits gain her patronage. She jogs round the park before breakfast, swims at lunchtime, plays tennis or squash in the evenings, does her stomach-control exercises at board-meetings and her five-minute daily maintainance programme last thing before she goes to bed. She pursues the burn and the glow avidly. She talks now of muscle tone rather than cellulite, and when she starts worrying about the incipient hint of lines around her eyes she wants rejuvenation through collagen implants instead of corrective face-lifts. She takes booster vitamins and eschews white bread, coffee, sugar and alcohol, which are no longer merely fattening, but are, much more evilly, unnatural poisons sneaking in to her system to ravage it. And only when she looks like a perfect specimen of an all-American twenty-year-old can she be said to have achieved true Superbeauty – so it's hardly surprising that she's still working on it.

Would-be Superwomen, needless to say, don't quite behave like this. Being born the wrong size or shape is a severe handicap to start with (and isn't it odd how few women *are* perfect size 10s at 5′10″ in their stockinged feet?), and if you're also unfortunate enough to lack a healthy glowing complexion and thick but manageable hair then you're probably out of the running. But you still try, experimenting with new shampoos, face cream, hair-styles and make-up at a cost of many hours of anxiety and a great deal of money – except that sometimes you forget or can't be bothered, and ruin the whole image by leaving your hair a day too long before washing, or missing out on make-up altogether: then you feel guilty about not making the effort, and try doubly hard for a few days before you lapse again. You may still wear those discreetly tasteful clothes, of course, and conceal your imaginary midriff bulge with long-line jackets and carefully cut skirts; you can spend a fortune on bras that promise to make you look more like Dolly Parton, or less; you can hide your lumpy ankles in baggy boots, or emphasize your swan-like neck with soft ruffles – but somehow there will still be days when you look and feel terrific, others when you know you're a frump, and others when you *thought* you looked and felt terrific until the first person you met said 'What's the matter with you, you look *ghastly*!'

You don't seem to lead the same sort of life as Superwoman does, in which her perfect fingernails are miraculously protected from typewriters, Sabatier knives, screwdrivers, badly designed food packets or awkwardly shaped parcels; her hems never get caught on vicious desk drawers and certainly never, like yours, when they're supposed to be innocently hanging up in the wardrobe. Your tights get snagged too, and splashed with muddy water by malicious passing taxis at the first sign of rain; your make-up never seems to achieve the same effect twice; buttons mysteriously disappear as you blink, and by the time you notice it's too late to iron another shirt (the one you want is *never* efficiently ready for you), or your other suit is at the cleaners. Hairdryers either sullenly refuse to work at all, or develop a life of their own and decide you're going to look like Rod Stewart when you were aiming for Princess Di. Dungarees on you somehow suggest the plumber's mate rather than a sexy androgene. And though you start your many diets with the best of intentions something always gets in their way, like an office party, a business lunch, a distraught friend in need of an encouraging drink, his rare and not to be rejected offer of dinner – or if it doesn't, as often as not you get so depressed at only having lost two pounds instead of three by the third day that you give it up as a failure anyway. You *meant* to jog every morning, but the temptation to have the extra half-hour in bed proved irresistible; the swimming pool is so sordid and over-chlorinated you can't bear it; the exercise class is so full of women who look like Jane Fonda already that your inferiority complex gets the better of itself and you don't go back; there's nobody to play tennis with now that Natasha's moved, and booking a squash court at a possible time takes about a day's serious application. Of course you *prefer* brown bread anyway, but white was all they had left; you need that cup of coffee to keep you going, and sugared it in the hope of an instant glucose buzz; you know you should give up smoking, but your life is so stressful at the moment you can't think about it just yet, and one glass won't hurt you . . . And then, of course, when you stand in deep depression in front of your mirror – which was specially refracted to magnify all bad points – you know the fact you've failed your body-image test is *all your own fault*.

Superwoman may not state it quite so obviously these days, but she certainly hasn't lost sight of the fact that a woman is still judged by her appearance before her actions – and for at least one very good reason. Traditionally, man has obtained and wielded power through either mental or physical superiority, whereas woman has done so through the manipulation of man with her sexual charms: in a world where we're still a long way from achieving an equal power base using man's armoury, who's going to be foolish enough to relinquish the weapons she's already got? And there are a great many other less rational causes for our behaviour too, like habit, or straightforward oneup womanship, or our persistent belief that our aim is still simply to catch the man; and so we will continue to be judged on appearances because we continue to believe in the validity of such judgements, and tailor our behaviour accordingly. Even though we know perfectly well that beauty is only skin deep, that it's what's in our minds that matters, and though it's idealogically unsound to *admit* we want to turn every room we enter into a bedlam of swooning males and snarling females, we still *do* want it. And we are still just as quick as men with the one-liner character assassination through physical disparagement, because somewhere in our muddled brains we genuinely believe that if we aren't beautiful, then we aren't sexually attractive and therefore we aren't 'nice' – because if every man really loves a good woman, why do they fall over themselves for that little hussy who has nothing to recommend her but the obvious availability of her body? The interchangeability of the words 'beautiful', 'attractive' 'nice' and now 'sexy' to describe something we like or approve of demonstrates the strength of the belief, just as the Soviet ideology is clearly proclaimed in the Russian language, where 'beautiful' and 'red' are the same word. But we're free to think the Russian example is absurd, not having yet decided that 'red' is 'sexy', while we don't even recognize the bias in our own language.

Perhaps in a subconscious attempt to justify her continuing obsession with her appearance in the face of the uncomfortably cogent feminist arguments against it, Superwoman has subtly shifted her emphasis over the past few years. Now she concentrates much more on the inner beauty of physical health and fitness than on the window-dressing of clothes and make-up: although the aim is still more to look wonderful than to be fit, harping on the health aspect not only makes it all right to crave a body beautiful, but can even give the firm impression that it's a positive social duty. Think of all the extra work you're giving your poor overloaded GP, or what disfavours your employer, what germs to your family and friends, as well as making life so much more difficult for yourself, if you don't bother to keep yourself at the peak of physical perfection the entire time! Of course you're tired, if you never take any exercise; you need to invest energy to gain it. A stomach bug raises the suspicion that you aren't eating the right food; colds and 'flu are a sure sign of bad living habits; how can you expect to feel well when you're lugging all that extra weight around? The promise of Jane Fonda and Victoria Principal and the rest is that if we follow their rules strictly we will be not only beautiful but radiantly well; the threat, if we don't, is that when we offend against their puritan standards of clean living we also call the curse of disease upon us. The cleverness in this fallacy is that 'health' incorporates the idea of not being ill, as well as this evangelistic new search for improvement, so that you can be made to feel doubly guilty on the grounds that you will have only yourself to blame if you are struck down by any malady from chicken-pox to cancer.

Apart from its meaning as not being ill, there is no absolute of health. *Our Bodies Ourselves* pointed out that 'tip-top health probably afflicts one in a thousand people': Helen Chappell, a lone dissenting voice amid the chorus of exercise tapes, quotes and expands this argument in *Company* (March 1984) to complain that 'a whole generation is being brought up to expect much, much more . . . (but) only the obsessive few are actually going to achieve this goal, and then only at a very high price. Ask yourself if you *really* want to live on All-Bran and jacket potatoes, drink Perrier water at parties, work out with weights for several hours a day.' The resounding answer from 99 per cent of the population would no doubt be 'no' – and yet the inclusion of the slim, the trim, the burn, the work-out or the glow under that health umbrella which also covers so much we are and should be concerned with, like the side-effects of aspirin, new cancer treatments, better perinatal care or the provisions for the elderly sick, leaves us with the uneasy conviction that whether we want to or not, we ought to. It's health, therefore it's medicine, and just like cough mixture or a visit to the dentist we don't expect it to be pleasant as well.

Yet what happens to the few who do achieve that one in

a thousand perfection? A top athlete, whose life revolves around and is subjugated to training to maintain a physical peak, can be incapacitated for weeks by the cold that might lay you low for a couple of days; if you turn an ankle, you may limp around in a crêpe bandage for a week or so, but a runner will be on crutches and off training for a matter of months; the 'wrong' diet could result in you in a scattering of spots or the odd queasy sensation, while it can reduce his or her fitness by an alarming percentage. These ones in a thousand sacrifice a great deal more than a glass of wine at a party to the ideal of perfect fitness, but they are aiming for one sole end in doing so: not only is there simply not room in any normal life for that sort of dedicated training, but your life neither needs nor can function properly with such fine tuning. It would be like expecting a Formula I car to cope with commuting – highly wasteful, and a lot less efficient than a Mini. And already warning voices are beginning to murmur about the dangers of pursuing the burn too assiduously without proper medical supervision, or the physical damage aerobic exercise can inflict on muscles not already highly-toned: although some of this alarmism can be written off as the natural cautious pessimism of the medical profession, the much-publicized dangers of anorexia or the example of the athletes suggest that there is probably a grain or two of truth in it.

Half-way between the healthy duty of physical fitness and the unholy desire for sex appeal lies slimming. Not only does this topic fill a fair proportion of the general women's media, but it actually has a number of high-circulation magazines devoted to it and it alone, while the books of and on diets or specifically slimming exercises still far outnumber the Fondas and Principals. A slim figure has been desirable in Western eyes (apart from a few Rubensesque excursions into the baroque delights of mountainous flesh) at least since the Greeks – and of course the Greek ideal of beauty was firmly based on the male body, not the female. There are cultures where the fatter a woman is, the more highly-prized, where the huge-bellied Earth Mother, potently fertile and promising of unimaginable riches, still holds sway, but the Western world is not among them. And despite the fact that there are perfectly good biological reasons for a woman to carry more fat than a man, despite the fact that many men find plump women more attractive than boylike ones, women don't; and we impose, to a great extent, our preferences on men as well as on ourselves. Whether this is through a transference of what we find sexually appealing in a man to what we imagine he will therefore find attractive in us, whether it is through a mistaken belief that if we look like them we will be treated like them, or whether it's just plain masochism, we slim fanatically in our thousands, vigorously punishing every hint of a curve and pinching viciously at any spare millimetre of flesh until we've bullied it into submission.

To an extent we're right, of course, just as to an extent 'the peak' is a sensible goal. But as with the peak of health, so with the shape and weight of our bodies – we've lost all sense of proportion in pursuit of a non-existent absolute. Floating in front of our eyes is the vision of the 5′10″ size 10; we don't stop to think that we might personally look like a concentration camp victim at size 10, or even to rationalize that we haven't fitted into anything smaller than a twelve since our early teens and are therefore unlikely to manage it now. In a species with a normal height range of almost eighteen inches, which has a variety of bone structures and muscle distribution to rival a supermarket's of cereals, it is absurd to try to impose three Euroweights or four Eurosizes of package. And it is even more absurd for women to impose this mental and physical torture on themselves, with only minimal encouragement from men and in the knowledge that it is a torture they have pledged themselves enthusiastically to eradicate. Fat may be a medical issue, but it really is a feminist one as well.

The unsurprising truth of the matter is that it's entirely

possible to be a normal, functioning, happy member of society without being a superfit model kit – in fact much more possible, since you'll actually have the time and energy to devote to your job, your family, your man, your hobbies, and all those other simultaneous parts of your life that you have and Superwoman doesn't, if you aren't wasting it all on the shell. Which doesn't mean to say that you have to put on a stone in weight on the grounds of liberation, or that you'll be happier with a pasty complexion, a shape like a sack of potatoes and a total inability to move more than three yards under your own steam than as a golden girl shining with vitality. It's still your body, which you live in, and just as it's natural to prefer one's home to be furnished and decorated in a style you like, so you will want yourself to be attractive as well: but you also require a home to be comfortably liveable in, and there are all too many people selling you the lie that appearances override ease, in flesh and blood as well as bricks and mortar. They don't.

It would be silly to set out to discourage you from keeping yourself healthy: up to a point it is a perfectly sensible and admirable aim. That point has been overreached when you no longer consciously *want* to do it – not the exercise itself, all exercises are boring at some point, but aim for the goal – but do it as a depressingly dutiful chore; when jogging may be good for you but you've begun to hate the sight of a track-suit, or your Jane Fonda exercise tape looms over you with all the enticement of maths homework. It would be equally silly to deny that a fit person may well be a less ill person – but infinitely more illness is caused by unhappiness and stress than by a couple of pounds overweight or a dull skin, and you run the risk of obsessing yourself into ill-health rather than out of it. So if fitness has become a chore for you, slimming a meaningless necessity not a means to an end, try the novel therapy of doing or eating what you want for a change, and just see what happens. You might discover that your body suits you better as a home than a prison.

All the more depressing, when you think about it, is the boring fact that the whole idea behind all this self-denial and self-immolation (apart from attracting those ideologically sound but ubiquitous men) seems to be to live longer. What for? – if you spend the first forty-odd years of your life denying yourself the things you enjoy, like cholestrol, or sleep, or any petty indulgence of that ilk, so that you can preserve yourself like a pickled walnut for an old age, denied any possibility of sexual attraction if you look more than twenty-five and even, now, knowing that you would be foolish to expect even respect, let alone concern or gratitude, from the arrogant, self-admiring young. Ageism is beginning to become a cult word in relation to employment, and tentatively to fashion design, but this new rebellion hasn't yet caused any noticeable dimunition in the adverts for magic potions and elixirs to keep your skin, hair and muscles looking 'young', 'dew- fresh' or 'soft as a baby's'.

And yet, as Helen Chappell argues (for a lone voice she covers a lot of wilderness), 'We don't *have* to find women in their forties or fifties so unattractive. We could quite easily find their facial lines interesting instead of ugly . . . We could see their character and experience as sexually attractive, as we do with men' (*Company*, April 1984). Or, to put it another way, 'Sure, it would be nice to look like Joan Collins at fifty – it would also be nice if it didn't matter that we looked like Sandy Gall!' (Maureen Lipman in *Options*, March 1984). Just because it is possible to look younger for longer these days shouldn't mean that the first grey hair or wrinkle puts you on the scrap heap. More important than elasticity of skin in the youth stakes is elasticity of mind, which is something the Superwoman generation actually has a good deal of (necessarily so, with all these contradictory new ideas and ideals clamouring for house room); if we could only push aside our preconceptions about absolutes in looks we might find that eighty- year-olds can be as mentally young and lively as eighteen-year-olds. Remember that a child actress can be 'too old' at fifteen, or a model at twenty-three, before you swallow any stories about landmarks on your face being irrevocable signs of middle age: remember too that 'the older man' really does believe in his increased physical distinction and sexual attractiveness, or that at thirteen you desperately wanted to be a sophisticated thirty. You wouldn't be human if you didn't feel the urge still to hold back the relentless march of age – but it's an old mentality you really fear, not the lived-in-face and body which are wrongly assumed to be its outward signs.

Even if you've accepted the impossibility, for you, of Daley Thompson's training programme, or a model body to work on, or of doing a Canute on the tide of lines and grey hairs, you will still inevitably want to disguise your bad features and emphasize your good ones with clever window-dressing in the form of carefully chosen clothes and make-up. Immediately, however, there is a confusion of goals, because you choose your style of appearance not simply to project yourself as an attractive woman, but also to project an image of the role you intend to play, and the two quite frequently clash or get mixed up with one another. If you're a blonde who looks great in electric blue, the sober beige suit which marks you down as a serious businesswoman will be at odds with the personality your psychological and sexual instincts are silently screaming to proclaim; the fun-loving theatrical you is uneasy in the Aran and tweed skirt of the mother-about-country; the vamp lurks warily beneath the discreetly Laura Ashley-ed bosom of the conformable director's wife, and the Earth Mother is uncomfortably confined in the skin-tight Vanderbilt jeans of the casually clued-up 'one of the boys, but with a difference'.

We have acquired a uniform mentality, learned from men and adopted in deference to the customs of their country, which sits badly with our fully-rounded, unpigeon-holed approach to life: far, far more than they, we want what we wear to announce the whole of what we are, and are frustrated by the rigid formulae of the City, the Law, the county or the disco at every turn. Men do suffer too from the archaic dress-codes that stifle their individuality, but only in rare cases; in general they delight in not only imposing the rules, but in obeying them too. It makes life so much easier, not to have the burden of deciding what to wear; a man 'knows where he is' when he can see with relief that he's in the same place as everyone else. Even the wildest extravagances of men in 'creative' jobs like advertising or design can be seen to conform to a model; it's a model of rebellion against all those blacks, greys and navys, but the pink and grey blouson jackets, two-tone shoes, graph-checked suitcase-style briefcases and canary-yellow sleeveless sweaters are as much a uniform as the other. He doesn't need to declare his personality through his clothes, because he's pretty confident of it: he does need to declare his profession, because during his working hours that *is* his identity – usually this means he will only be made miserable by conformity if he's in the wrong job. Much more difficult is the position of women, desperately determined to declare their individuality, their difference from men and from each other, at the same time as their fitness to take place in a man's world without causing too much upheaval.

In fact, the sky won't fall on your head if you wear scarlet at a board meeting (one of the toughest female company directors I ever came across had a penchant for vivid fuchsia, in which she looked stunning but certainly never gave anyone the impression she was frivolous) any more than it will if you appear at the disco in demure Victorian monochrome. Beyond the odd conservative enclave which demands skirt rather than trousers – and they also demand suits and ties for men, so they are non-sexist in their dictatorship – there isn't a sufficiently long tradition yet of women being assertively themselves for any hard and fast social rules to have built up around what we may and may not wear when, and with luck they never will. Because in this one area we are actually moderately successful: even the former tyrants of the fashion world have been reluctantly forced to concede that they will probably never again be able to dictate an overall 'look'. Discouraged, after years of insisting that the only possible garment this year is a black and white checked tent only to find themselves ignored by clouds of wantonly pastel-clad, neat-waisted women, they have now accepted the novel concept of variety in response to our nascent self-confidence. Within the confines of common sense, we are growing in the freedom to suit ourselves – obviously scruffy dungarees aren't suitable wear for your top client, nor are they going to impress the bank manager, the chairman or the new man in the same way as tailored chic or stunning sophistication will, but we know that from ordinary good manners and our own devious image-building aims, rather than from any sense of external imposition; and then whether you go for demure efficiency in grey or blinding impact in orange and black zig-zags is entirely up to you. If high heels and a pencil skirt are what you want to wear for a lazy day around the house, you may be being impractical but nobody can say you're positively wrong; if tailored clothes make you feel uncomfortably constricted, there are flowing lines to choose from instead; the liberation of discovering there is no law that says you must wear jeans at the weekends if you find skirts more comfortable, or vice versa, can be quite surprisingly life-enhancing. Even if you do have to dress formally for professional reasons, all sorts of small rebellions are available to you in the form of jewellery, silly hats, disconcerting belts, buttons and bows – they are only small, but they'll make you feel better for having made some sort of statement all the same. Instead of trimming your character to fit your clothes, you do have for the first time in history a genuine freedom to choose a wardrobe to suit your personality: it would be silly to deny yourself it.

Apart from the complex problem of dressing to fit an image, you can also worry quite satisfactorily for years about dressing to enhance your physical attractions, or more likely, disguise your failings – and there is folklore enough here to tyrannize the most mutinous of women. Waists will make you look shorter by breaking up the body line; bright colours will make you look like a barn door; you must confine yourself to vertical stripes to camouflage your lack of inches, and A-line skirts to hide your bulging hips; high heels fine down your ankles, soft ruffles your square jaw; blue brings out the colour of your eyes so they don't look so small, while green makes your complexion seem sallow. The same criteria and criticisms are levelled at your lank hair, your dry skin, your knobbly knees, hairy legs and untended fingernails as at your big nose or drooping bottom – what can't be changed or eradicated altogether must be disguised and hidden. And you will notice that the vast majority of fashion and beauty tips of this sort are concerned with negatives infinitely more than with positives: this could be out of a genuinely altruistic desire to give help where it is most needed, but it might also have something to do with our puritanical disapproval of admiring anything good in ourselves, or indeed with Superwoman's 'success is work' ethic.

The trouble is that a life of camouflage is as tedious as it is ultimately unproductive. When you catch the man, he's going to find out eventually that legs have to be shaved or waxed to stay hairless, or that under the size twelve exterior is a size fourteen bursting to get out, or that your eyes do look tiny without any make-up, don't they?: but he almost certainly won't run away screaming on that account. And if he does have the temerity to object, you could always point out his pot-belly, smelly feet, and liberally-dandruffed shoulders in return – however thoroughly you have absorbed the creed of woman as appearance, he certainly can't get away with it. Even those less favoured men, whose admiration you only require for the surface, are more likely to appreciate a joyous streak of colour or interest than a monotonously neutral facade: remember that after all, the purpose of camouflage is to avoid being seen, and its effects can very easily extend from your self-dictated bad points to cover the rest of you as well. The sum total of all those jug-handle ears, lumpy feet and thickened waistlines is you, not a tailor's dummy, so if you're going to feel wonderfully young and carefree in a scarlet sweater then forget your size 40 bust and wear it, or even flaunt it; the way you feel will show through in the way you look, and instead of disparaging comments about block-and-tackle you're more likely to be pleasantly surprised by the remarks on how good you're looking today. And because it is always yourself that you have to satisfy first, last and in the final analysis only, no amount of horizontal stripes are going to make you look like Hattie Jacques when you know in your heart you feel like Twiggy.

You already know all this, of course. Intellectually you are quite well aware that a lively mind is more attractive than a vacant Farrah Fawcett-clone face; that a radiant personality is more likely to be surrounded by friends and lovers than a ravishing idiot; that in any case it would be not only degrading to you but also immoral of you to *want* to be seen as a stereotyped sex symbol. But you don't have to stop washing your hair and wander around in indeterminately coloured sacks, wondering forlornly why you ever kidded yourself that men would have the wit to spot your inner beauty, to prove it. All you have to do is relax; stop working yourself into an anxiety state about the way you look, and though you may never rival Cleopatra, you'll be a much more attractive proposition to yourself and everyone else than the crabby character drawn with exhaustion from near-starvation diets and over-exercise, and permanently frowning in tension at the discomfort of too-tight clothes and perilous heels, which used to be you. If you can do that, then you will look good because you will want to look good and will believe that you do: and if you still have to admit that you're unlikely to set the town alight, well, that no longer matters to you anyway, does it?

# 9

## *The Organization Woman*

Just as there are grey areas of extra-curricular activity in the office, so there are outside it; and as in the office, so at home, they are almost always dealt with by women. They consist of the items that don't really count as anyone's responsibility because they don't really count at all, but which are actually phenomenally time-consuming when you stop and think about them. Making appointments with service engineers, writing thank-you letters, getting everyone invited to dinner on the same night, ringing doctors, dentists or vets, booking tables, paying the paper bill, checking timetables – it's a curious phenomenon of the most otherwise equal partnerships that these tasks (which a paid employee would rightly resent being expected to do) are resignedly accepted by the woman as her inevitable lot; and even if you're single, the betting is that you have more than once found yourself undertaking them for friends or flatmates.

The chief annoyance about them is that they take up so much time without producing any tangible results. It's easy enough, in theory, to ring the gas, or electricity, or telephone companies to report an out-of-order appliance and arrange for it to be mended: in practice it can take half a day, first waiting for the phone to be answered, then being put through to the right department for your area or problem, then trying to explain what the matter is, then trying even harder and with less success to suggest that you would like a clearer idea of when they're coming than 'towards the end of the week' or 'before 1pm'. It sounds simple just to 'get a man in' to mend the washing machine – but finding out who services your make of machine in your area can and frequently does turn into a major research project. Booking tables isn't quite a straightforward matter of picking up the phone, dialling the number, and giving the name and time: first they don't answer, then they don't understand you, then they're full anyway and you have to start the whole process again. And who in their right mind attempts to ring up for theatre tickets without at least a certain two hours to spare? Writing your own thank-you letters is enough of a chore, but to be responsible for his and the children's as well is adding insult to injury, and why on earth should you know the date of his mother's birthday better than he does? The shopping list, and the mental or physical tally of what you're running out of rears its head here too, as does the supernatural ability, assumed in all women, to know exactly where to lay her hands on anything from the radiator key, to his passport, to that book by someone with a funny name which had that interesting chapter on fungi, to the receipt for the five-year-old cooker, to the baking powder. Although none of these niggling little activities can in itself be glorified with the name of a job, added together they have no difficulty at all in amounting to an irritating and frustrating day's work – and work made more irritating and frustrating by the feeling at the end of it that you haven't actually *done* anything concrete at any rate. And if you do find yourself trying to explain to a man just how you've been spending your day, the frustration will be compounded many times over by his inability to understand how on earth *that* could have occupied you for so long.

For anyone living alone, the organization of living is more or less inevitable, though the vast majority of single men will almost certainly have a back-up team of women, from mothers, to neighbours, to their staff, to ex-girlfriends to call on in a real emergency. And if you have a live-in-man – and therefore, theoretically, a choice – it's reasonably easy to see why you still land yourself with the responsibility. As a would-be Superwoman you know that all grey areas are your province anyway; you accept immediately that you *can* do it, and are less likely to be concerned with why you should than with why you don't seem to have got the hang of doing it with the streamlined efficiency of Superwoman. Both your Superwoman ambitions and your feminist principles then combine to ensure that you aren't averse to proving your superiority to mere men through your organizational talents; your Earth Mother instinct connives with this sexually competitive streak in you by encouraging you to believe that your child/man needs protection against a nasty, rough world in which he is unfitted to fend for himself, and your historical perception of your subservient feminine role reinforces this protective tendency by leading you to avoid bothering him with trifles unworthy of his attention. One way and another, you expect to 'manage' – and manage you will, especially as you know full well that if you did force him to agree to do any of these jobs they'd simply go undone.

What is less easy to understand is your man's attitude to the whole business, because his reasons are based on a complex collection of assumptions at least as broadly-based as yours but less conveniently labelled, and are further complicated by the apparent truth that, whether he's an old-school chauvinist or a fully paid-up human being, he still reacts the same way: he just doesn't seem to notice that there's anything inequitable about any of it. But equally, he reacts in three different ways to different kinds of organizational problem: he either can't possibly do it himself (he's much too busy, or he doesn't know the number), or 'you'll know what to say to them', or it doesn't need doing. His fourth line of defence is that you're making a fuss about nothing and it's all perfectly simple – and if you're foolhardy enough to stand over him while *he* phones the garage or the Electricity Board, sod's law will instantly come into action and prove him miraculously, triumphantly right: he will then have shown conclusively that you are only being feeble, and will never have to bother proving it again.

Partly, of course, it's his taking-cover technique coming

into play again: if some would-be Superwoman is daft enough to take these boring tasks off his shoulders he's certainly not daft enough to argue with her: he is much more likely to encourage her by starting off so badly that she takes over, or by pointing out winningly how good you are at that sort of thing. And partly, it's his inbred expectation of female support-systems for his male-topped pyramid. The office parallel is very clear in this respect, for indeed the life-organization tasks would fit quite aptly into a secretarial or PA's job description: correspondence, appointments, filing, office administration, back-up research and the challenging opportunity for some decision-making – or, to put it the way so many disillusioned secretary/PAs do, 'running around after him like a mother hen'. The man whose secretary is temporarily absent will wander around pathetically unable to do any administrative work at all, because he can't find anything, or has forgotten how to look up and dial a phone number; nor will he find anything odd in asking for help from an overworked, equal female colleague: even the newly-emergent man who has only marginally more hopes of getting a secretary than his female counterpart, or at least hasn't got one yet, still really expects someone – that is, some woman – to shield him from these excursions into the tedious business of everyday living. The assumption doesn't transfer from office to home, however, but the other way round: it's not that he sees all women as secretaries so much as that he sees all secretaries as women, and therefore as having the clear function of keeping his affairs in order.

But these aren't by any manner of means the only roots of his non-organization: they certainly couldn't be applied to the average intelligent, female-orientated younger man, who would only need to have them pointed out to him to be immediately horrified at the inequity of the position. There is a further element in the different attitudes of the sexes towards the home and by extension the apparatus therein, born again out of your respective roles as breadwinner and homemaker, but none the less real for that – he requires the place to function adequately as a service station for his use, but beyond that he recognizes it as your territory. Thus it is immediately obvious that anything that malfunctions or gets misplaced within the home is your responsibility, and he could even go further and persuade himself he would be guilty of unwarrantable interference if he attempted to share that responsibility with you. (Surprisingly, perhaps, this sensitivity for your preserves doesn't automatically extend to surface maintenance like housework or decorating, or to the radical financial questions of the mortgage and the service bills, and it certainly doesn't stop him from complaining vociferously if you fail to live up to his standards of maintenance either.) And with certain niggling repair jobs he genuinely won't see what you're going on about – what does it matter if the telephone's guts have all spilled out, as long as it still works; if one of the circuits keeps blowing, why go to the potential expense and trouble of rewiring when you can just carry on mending the fuse; or if the hoover needs an overhaul, why not buy a new one and have done? In some areas so much more dependent on order around them than the more adaptable female of the species, men have an extraordinary capacity in others for living happily in a botched-up make and mend environment that at times verges on the Heath-Robinson.

A man who will obligingly pay all bills, happily write out cheques in supermarkets, and even, with only a little persuasion, take cats to vets, children to doctors, and wait in for service engineers, can still show a marked reluctance to make any of the appointments or arrangements for these activities or to walk into the local newsagent and pay for the newspapers. This is quite patently not simply his inherent chauvinism getting the better of him, since that would preclude his having anything to do with them at all: it is at least partly because he'd have to *speak* to people. Men, so sure of their place in the sun when protected by the armour of their job title and the society of their peers, are much less self-confident than women when their part isn't clearly scripted for them: the same disinclination to probe the minds of others which makes them so eminently clubbable also makes them shy away from non-professional or peer-group human contact in a way that women find as difficult to understand as men do our ability to spend an hour calling the builder. Many men talk freely for hours to a perfect stranger met in a bar, yet panic totally at the possibility of having to pass the time of day with a neighbour or the milkman – my father used to refuse point-blank to visit a certain shop because 'they know me, so I have to *talk* to them!' Moreover, man has an automatic uncertainty about decision-making outside his own carefully circumscribed sphere, a fundamental insecurity fostered by generations of women screaming '*Wednesday*? But you *know* Helena and Chris are coming on Wednesday, how could you be so *stupid*?' (which he did know, but the knowledge was in a different pigeonhole from the one marked 'Car service' so the two didn't connect, and now he's made himself look an idiot, which he doesn't like one little bit and which only makes him resentfully inclined to snap back 'Well do it yourself next time!'). Few men enjoy making decisions at the best of times – the ones who do tend to be either millionaires or bankrupts – and his general unformulated wariness about any possible unpleasantness can do much towards paralyzing him into total inactivity in the business of making small ones.

And it is undeniable that patience with the petty irritations of life is not a conspicuously male virtue – perhaps because they've managed to avoid so many of them they aren't used to coming across such rubs in their way, or perhaps it's the other way round. A man who can face with stoic calm such major calamities as a stove-in nearside wing, a lost contract, or possibly even, on a good day, Spurs losing as home; who can spend hours twiddling and teasing at a finicky piece of electrical work or at getting the figures absolutely accurate, will slam the phone down in a fury when it's unanswered on the fourth ring, or explode with irritation against an innocent machine for having the temerity to fall terminally ill after ten years of alternate neglect and abuse. (This can extend to women too – you may be guilty of extraordinary inconsideration, not to say lèse-majesté, if you catch 'flu: he, of course, is dying.)

Some and in some degree all of these conditions, needless to say, apply to some and in some degree all men in their division of the organizational labour with women, and some and in some degree all women respond by taking over the responsibility as much to save trouble as to further their own complicated motives. And it is women with partners who are guilty of the wanton assumption of work in this area, since if you are single you aren't so much in the Superwoman Trap as in a simple necessity trap. Both of you, however, have the same ultimate problem in that you still need to cope with these boring practicalities in the least time-consuming way possible.

Superwoman, of course, has a filing cabinet in her kitchen drawer which contains a complete dossier on every appliance in the house, copies of her Christmas card lists for the past fifteen years, a constantly updated survey of all regular maintenance work required or undertaken, and a neatly-docketed cache of passports, birth certificates, NHS cards, and all the other documentation necessary in a free state; her family diary contains careful notes of all birthdays and anniversaries (transferred from last year's on Boxing Day in the intervals between writing thank-you letters), meticulous details of all dental appointments, car tax renewal dates and other immovable feasts of that sort, and she also writes in, in different colours of ink, all the family's social engagements; she has a checklist of important telephone numbers on the wall by the phone, including everyone from doctor to picture restorer, with notes of opening hours and reference numbers where necessary: Superwoman can therefore plan her life with military precision in no time flat, and take emergencies effortlessly in her stride. This unexciting but worthy efficiency does presuppose, however, that she has unlimited time available to wait for service engineers and harrassed medical secretaries to answer their telephones; that she will be at home with access to all these ready-reference tools at a time when shops, offices or surgeries are prepared to talk to her; and that her family are as tidy-minded as she, or at least co-operative to the extent of telling her what they're doing next Thursday week – unless these three basic conditions are met, the system quickly collapses.

And for the rest of us, the system is probably on the verge of collapse, if not in total ruin, even without our inability to meet those conditions. The one vital phone number turns out to have missed transfer from your old address book, or is on a scrap of paper somewhere waiting to be written in; the name and birthdate of Sonia and Jim's latest is on their Christmas card, which you know you kept, but you don't know where; you're going to have to ring the plumber from work, but you haven't got a note of his number when you get there; appointments in your office diary don't find their way into the home one, or in his diary don't find their way into yours. Any permutation of these possible communication breakdowns, combined with the remarkable talent of children for losing the cyclostyled sheet of school dates on the way home, and of your acquaintances for changing their plans without reference to yours, can bring chaos round your ears in an instant. What's more, whatever anyone says about organization freeing more of your time, there are occasions when the immediate imperatives are such that it comes very low on your list of priorities; like cleaning out the cupboard under the sink, it's the sort of job that most normal people tend to reserve for a determined assault on a rainy day, rather than to tackle immediately in between the washing up and the ironing.

Obviously a certain amount of efficiency with paperwork is a good thing: but just as with all good things, you can have too much of it. It's fine if you have someone else to do it for you, but to try for Superwoman-style records can actually take almost as long as to waste such time as you currently do on looking for things; to try to add the skills of an archivist to all the other Superskills you juggle with may well be asking too much of yourself. It's an exact science at the best of times, and therefore not at all simple to combine successfully with simultaneous demands on your attention, and if you do get it wrong because you're distracted, or in a hurry, you risk losing vital information more certainly than if you'd just left it quietly on the back of an envelope on your dressing table in the first place. Ask any clerk what they find most frustrating about taking over a new job, and at least half of them will launch into a diatribe about eccentric or plain inaccurate filing systems, or mistyped telephone numbers: you can search for the carpet cleaner's details until you're blue in the face if you've filed them under 'house' instead of 'decor' or 'Betterclean' instead of 'carpet', while at least if they're still in that pile in the bedroom they stand a chance of surfacing sooner or later. And it may be a waste of time to spend half an hour searching for the garage's number, but if you've carefully filed and transferred it for four years from list to list, the upholsterer's address is going to have taken you up more time, unproductively, when you next come to use it after a four-year gap only to find he's gone out of business so you have to start all over again anyway. In as far as the filing, you should forget about visions of a bright red filing cabinet and simply aim, by whatever method seems best, but preferably one that ensures there is only one place you have to look, to be reasonably sure of your chances of finding what you need if not promptly, then at least at all.

With birthdays, anniversaries and appointments you only really have two choices: write them in your diary or forget them. You can't rely on your memory to cope all the time, especially when it's got so much else to do; so don't be tempted to believe that John's birthday is etched on your heart, because one day it'll rub off. A birthday book won't do at all, unless you are organized enough to check it every week (and if you're that organized you don't need any helpful suggestions anyway), but even then it provides an additional routine which you don't need: everything should be in one place so you can see it all at once – unless you have an office diary as well, in which case it should be in both places so you see it all at least twice and it's wherever you happen to be when you're about to go and buy a card, or telephone the vet or whatever. And having written all these vital things into your diary, do remember to look at it: it's astonishing how easy it is not to, under the happy but erroneous delusion that by writing something in you've actually done all you need to do about it . . . And unless you are completely laid-back about the idea of your man or your flatmate walking in in the middle of a dinner-party they'd forgotten was happening (assuming that they haven't been co-opted into the preparation, which if they're getting to eat the results they should have been); or about being told at eight in the morning that you're expected to be playing business-wife at a dinner the same evening; or about never managing to get a holiday arranged at all, or arranging it so it clashes with the school exams, then you must also go in for the business of cross-checking and cross-entering: as soon as other people get involved, even the most organized person's plans can go haywire.

You might consider forgetting some of the birthdays and anniversaries in any case. It sounds a bit cavalier, and many people do genuinely like to remember these occasions for all their circle – but an awful lot of people don't bother very much about them. You can't very well abandon your immediate family to agelessness, you probably don't want to ignore close friends, and Christmas, birthdays and anniversaries are an important formula for keeping in more or less regular touch with those you rarely see, but do you really need to mark punctiliously every personal landmark of your dozen-casual-meetings-a-year friends, many of whom are as likely to respond with blank astonishment as with gratification at being so favoured? It seems reasonable to decide that with this range of your acquaintance it's nice if you do remember, but will hardly be remarked if you don't, and certainly can't be seen as a dereliction of duty or a cause for social opprobium. To be quite brutal about it, how many of them remember yours?

In the same category as birthdays come correspondence, dental and medical check-up appointments, and invitations: all decidedly female jobs. Everyone has to write some letters, whether to lonely elderly relations or to far-flung friends, whether they are long screeds of stream of consciousness or brief dutiful notes; everyone needs dental visits from time to time, and if you aren't going to be a hermit then it follows that from time to time invitations must be issued: if you enter into any of these ventures jointly with a man, however, he will not be included in 'everyone' on this occasion. Letters and invitations (telephone invitations literally) come under the class of 'talking to people' as well as being secretarial functions in any case. And if you have children, then the unenviable post of first scribe, then supervisor, is automatically yours – not only is it a female job, but they're 'your' children as well.

The trick with letters is that they are of two sorts: the ones that say something specific, and the conversational ones that exchange news and chat, and both of them tend to get put off because they both in their different ways seem to demand an enormous effort. You forget, when faced with a long list of thank-you letters, that each recipient is only going to see one of them and so won't appreciate that you've spent twenty minutes racking your brain for alternative wordings of the phrase that has become so boring to you; and you rarely consider that your best friend in Kuala Lumpur might prefer to get a letter now, however short, than to wait three months for thirty pages of autobiography. We tend to see letter-writing, in our telecommunication age, either as a formal duty ('office stuff') and therefore intimidating, or as a self-indulgent pleasure and therefore to be put off until the chores are done. You may indeed, if you think about it, find some of your private letters, just like some of your business ones, could easily be replaced by a phone call which doesn't somehow carry the same portentous aura about it; but had you also considered that a pretty postcard will be just as welcome in place of others, and leaves you less blank paper to feel obliged to fill? The long chatty letters can often be written in instalments, diary-style; you must also convince yourself, if you're in doubt, that insofar as they serve to keep your friendships in repair they are quite as necessary to the organization of your life as the dutiful ones, if not more so, and so are not an unwarrantable indulgence at all. And while there is probably very little hope of persuading your man to supervise the children's letters, or to do more than scrawl a sentence or his signature on the bottom of his own, you stand a better chance of striking a bargain with him whereby you do the writing and he stamps and posts them: going to the post-office doesn't, paradoxically enough, seem to involve him in the terrors of communication, and it relieves you at least of the most time-sensitive part of the job.

Written invitations can be shared out once you've provided a list of names and the master text, but telephonic ones are frequently safer under your control, since they otherwise tend not to get issued. Again, they can sometimes seem to be guilty pleasures rather than efficient organizational calls, simply because the people you're ringing are presumably friends: you just have to be stern with yourself and settle down with the telephone – but be stern with yourself, too, about keeping your mind on the matter in hand rather than spending three-quarters of an hour catching up on the gossip with each of them. They're in the same boat as you are, so they won't take offence. And as for dental and medical appointments – I suspect that a large part of men's reluctance to make them is based on their reluctance to keep them: if yours is as well, you will be automatically inclined to put them off and so turn the making of the appointment into the problem. Looking on the bright side, this should lighten your attitude to the appointment itself when you do arrange it, but by and large you have to be big and brave and swallow the nasty medicine as quickly as possible.

All this is a long way from the most immediate problems of maintenance organization: the endless round of insurance queries, calls to repairmen and battles with delivery people which can knock your whole life off balance. These are the real confidence-killers, since the very fact of having to deal with them at all suggests that something has already happened to put your fragile framework out of true, and this is in part what makes them so irritating to handle: isn't it enough that you've spent half the morning mopping up the washing machine's overflow, or a day without any hot water or the use of the car, or hundreds of pounds for a replacement sofa, without having to put up with further hassles to get the first one righted? For a true Trap-ee, already nervously aware that her dream castle is built on shifting sand, the initial reaction borders on entirely disproportionate despair at the sight of the edifice crumbling around her, and she knows immediately that only further erosion can result from her efforts with uncaring bureaucrats, fully-booked engineers, or a malevolently-inclined telephone system. The only conceivable value of this reaction is that at least if she does get through first time to a helpful repairer – and gets an early appointment, which is not at all the same thing – or finds a shop that will deliver on a Saturday, she will be pleasantly reassured to find everything so much easier than she expected: it is regrettably more likely, however, that all her worst fears will be realized, which will increase her tension, and so diminish her ability to face the ensuing annoyances reasonably.

British suppliers and repair and maintenance companies are by and large appallingly cavalier towards their customers; private firms less so than the large monopolies, but none of them by any manner of means wonderful. First there is the impersonal indifference of the switchboard operators who, you are convinced, by the time you have rung , unanswered, for six minutes by your watch, leave you to stew first before they answer and then in mid-air while they're 'trying to connect you' for the sheer malicious fun of it. Then there is the smug finality of the bureaucratic 'No, I'm sorry, I can't guarantee a day or time'; and then, when the engineer finally arrives a week later at a totally different time from the one you'd dragged reluctantly out of the office (so you're quite possibly out) he hasn't got the right parts – though you carefully explained what was wrong – or he announces with ill-concealed satisfaction that you have got a really nasty one there: then you have to face the repulsive prospect of arranging another three visits and paying an astronomical bill into the bargain, as well as continuing without the use of your hot water/telephone/washing machine or whatever for a further indefinite but doubtless prolonged period. Similarly, if you take your car, watch, vacuum cleaner or any other vital appliance into a shop or garage, they will have to order the parts, or have got a very full order-book at the moment, or don't do that model, or claim it's irreparable and you'll need to buy a new one: it's no wonder we tend to expect the worst, when that's what we so often get.

The service industries in particular often appear to be part of the giant conspiracy to keep women in their place – that is, the home. They're free to continue to claim that they can't institute an appointments system – which nevertheless seems to work quite well for the rest of the world – if they know that in most households some poor woman can rearrange or temporarily halt her entire schedule to fit in with their convenience: I'd like to think that with a few more years of women demanding first call so they can get into work some time that morning this might eventually change, but in view of the declining figures for female employment I rather doubt it. I did once spend some time explaining to a woman at the Gas Board that she shouldn't find it so surprising that I was out of the house since she obviously was as well, but it was uphill work and she still didn't sound totally convinced (and after that I got consistently put through to people who didn't seem to understand a word I said): if even working women believe that other women should be at home to wait on the convenience of working men, what hope have we got? And when you are allowed to speak to 'the man' himself, it appears incomprehensible why he should have gone into that job in the first place, since he doesn't seem to approve of any of the appliances under his charge, or want to repair them at all if he can avoid it, or indeed if so many of them are, according to him, irreparable. The consumer magazines say that built-in obsolescence is going out of fashion for the machinery itself, but it still seems at times to be firmly in favour with the workforces who should welcome its disappearance. And as for the retailers – perhaps they never told their employees that they were in the business of selling things, judging from their frequent marked reluctance to do anything to further such an eccentric aim.

There isn't an awful lot you can do about much of this. You can arrive at the office half an hour earlier, so you can sit down and wait for your call to be answered without panicking about what else you should be doing instead, and when it is answered you could try remembering that the operator only took so long because every other woman in thc country is doing the same as you, and she only sounds bored because she *is* bored – it's nothing personal. You can insist, politely, on first call even if it means you have to wait a week, or you can swallow your fury and admit to yourself that you could perfectly well work from home on Tuesday morning; or you could lumber your homebound neighbour instead (though this is unsatisfactory unless the job to be done is completely straightforward); or you can get yourself marked down as 'difficult', which may result in appointments being made and kept or might have exactly the opposite effect, so requires considerable forethought and an element of gambling.

If you have a non-organizational man, you could agree

to make the date if he keeps it, but you must then be as careful of his convenience as you would be of your own, and even then he can easily produce an emergency meeting, real or invented, when the time comes. Conversely, if he leaves you to deal with the organization, you should make it quite clear that he has thereby forfeited any right to question whatever action you instigate: there is no position more uncomfortable than that of mediator between the workman who tells you one thing, and the man who scornfully tells you it's nonsense – Scylla and Charibdis were a doddle by comparison. It's surprisingly easy to forget, when you're acting on his behalf over his car, or the new boiler he's going to pay for, that if he really feels that strongly about it he can handle the negotiations himself, and even harder to tell him so: yet the response, when I finally did it, was complete acceptance after only a very short bout of astonishment. And if he's one of those who has proved that organizing anything is simple, then so's your answer: if he finds it so simple, and you find it so exasperating, he can do it. (He will then, of course, blithely arrange for the MOT to be done and the carpet to be laid while he's away in Amsterdam on business, and you're up to your eyeballs with a major project, and you will have to rearrange everything to conform to possibility and next time you'll be back where you started – doing it yourself.) Or you can simply ignore the problem completely, and pretend you don't mind washing in cold water or walking two miles to the station, in the hope that your nerves will outlast his: they probably won't, though, and you'll kick yourself for not having just got the thing done straight away.

Beyond any of these measures, ranging from the drastic to the trivial, all you can really do is to accept the inevitability of frustration – but try to accept it calmly rather than with mounting tension, and then it really *won't* be as bad as you thought. With individual suppliers, of course, you can quite easily become friends by dint of spending five minutes listening to a petal-by-petal description of their prize dahlias, or giving them whatever small job you can to keep your name and custom in mind for when you need a favour: then you should be saved any major problems in that field at least until they move or go out of business. And the only other thing you should consciously try to do is to treat all household breakdowns as emergencies, and make that dreaded initial phone call immediately. Whether you're at home or at work, it's all too easy not to get round to it, either because you can do it in half an hour when you've finished washing up, or because you've got to do something else first to meet a deadline: whole weeks can go by in this way, with the task assuming more terrifying proportions, and more evidence of your own inadequacy, all the time.

You will never achieve Superwoman's formidable standards of organization unless you work on it for far too long to be organizationally rational, and since you have all your other lives to lead as well, that would be to let the means supersede the end. You do need to go some way with her in setting up foolproof reference systems, but you don't need to frighten yourself or anyone else by letting them become a fetish and reduce you to a pattern-card of perfect organization without a spark of spontaneity left in you. Life may be rather more haphazard, and occasionally more uncomfortable, if you lack her forethought and ready-prepared crisis routine, but it can be a lot less dreary too.

And take comfort from this thought: no amount of organization can prevent the occasional mechanical crisis; and since conveniences such as hot water, her car, or her telephone are the very lifeblood of Superwoman's organization, she is probably worse off without them than any human being – including you. It may be unworthy – but it's wonderfully reassuring to think of Superwoman being knocked from her pedestal once in a while.

# 10

## *Woman Driver*

You'd think that anyone would be reasonably satisfied with a successful career, fulfilling motherhood, stunning romantic and sex life, professional cooking and hostly skills, and a genius for administration. Most people, you might feel, would be content to be completely confident of one of these attributes, and would believe they had done well to cope more or less competently with all of them. You may think it's impossible that anyone could attempt more. In which case, I'm afraid, I've got bad news for you: these are just the basics. To be a true Superwoman, you have to go a long, long way further.

Having mastered the basics, Superwoman still has free time lying heavy on her hands. She fills these unforgiving minutes with a variety of activities, designed either to help maintain her overall efficiency, or for economy, or to keep alive old-fashioned womanly arts (her Earth Mother instinct), or to increase her self-sufficiency in traditionally masculine areas, or simply for the fun of it. She has done a course in car maintenance – or at the very least learnt how to change a tyre, charge a battery and adjust the spark plugs – and she may be starting to talk about taking the Advanced Driving Test too. Decorating is almost the first thing she turns her hand to; indeed, she even considers it as a natural and integral part of the housework, and from paint and paper it is only a small step to carpentry and electrics, though she probably doesn't attempt these on any very ambitious scale. Her sewing isn't confined to the hem repair and button replacement sort, but encompasses talents for everything from evening clothes to curtains, and she knits Arans, Fair Isles and Patricia Roberts designs with equal speed and facility. She went to upholstery classes and puts her studies to good effect, finding a Chesterfield no more intimidating than a dining chair, and is thus able to demonstrate her flair for interior design better too, since she can claim that when she saw the material she just *knew* it would be perfect, and then of course had to do it herself (the emphasis then remains on her taste in choosing the fabric, as well as spilling over into her skill in making it up). As well as maintaining the garden as a decorative extension of the house, she also uses it as a source of raw materials for the exotica she delights, in her Superprovider role, in whipping out of her larder or freezer like rabbits from a hat. Her herbs are always fresh from the garden, as are her new vegetables; she may never succeed in growing an avocado fruit on the plant she has carefully nurtured from a stone balanced on two pins above a glass of water, but if she doesn't it will be the climate's fault, not hers; she prides herself on her bottled and frozen fruits, homemade jams and jellies, and especially on her gallons of tomato chutney, made to use up the glut of fruits from her thriving tomato plantation. Her home would in effect compare favourably in terms of produce with a sizeable eighteenth-century estate.

Superwoman derives enormous satisfaction from all these sorts of tasks, not only because they represent vast range of Superskills in themselves but also because they somehow contribute to her rather muddled ideal of a 'real' and 'natural' lifestyle. The Earth Mother/Homemaker in her has always been the strongest element in her make-up, so that she admires and yearns to emulate the image of a more gracious age, when a woman could truly be seen as the benificent provider, serene in the command of her household and glorious in her generosity. What she completely fails to take into account is that no serene householder ever attempted to come to terms with the 'basics' of a career and motherhood as well, let alone making her own preserves without having help with the dirty work, and certainly never had to contend with the vagaries of the internal combustion engine or ready-pasted wallpaper. She made chair covers so the chairs would be comfortable to sit on, and curtains to keep out the draughts; her home-made produce was home-made because that was the only way she could get or afford it, not because it was in some mysterious way more 'valid'.

There is absolutely no logical reason to suppose that there is any particular virtue in doing jobs you can legitimately avoid; and to take on jobs that don't need to be done at all, let alone by you, for any motive that causes you to consider them *as* jobs rather than as hobbies, is rank madness. Self sufficiency in suburbia is a pointless aim, being both simply unnecessary and in any case ultimately impossible to achieve – try telling the gas, electricity or water boards that you no longer require their services, and see what a baffled outcry there is. Since you're supposed to be liberating yourself from the tyranny of your history, it would be silly to reject the facilities for doing so that the modern age has to offer, like supermarkets, convenience foods, carpet-laying services, washing machines and food processors: of course there are often times when you want to do something yourself, and there are old-fashioned crafts you can master reasonably easily with the help of today's appliances, but if you're on an 'I'm inadequate unless I go back to the real values' kick, remember that the real values concerned were nesessarily achieved without all these household aids while still demanding the products of them. People used to make nettle soup not because it was a particular delicacy, but because nettles were a free and freely available substitute for other, grander vegetables; they bottled fruits and pickled things and preserved meats so they would be sure of having something to eat in the lean months; they learned how to ply a needle or a chisel because they couldn't afford either to buy new articles or to employ someone else to ply on their behalf: it was then a virtue to be a good manager in a way that, with our higher standard of living and improved food production techniques, is no longer applicable today. What Superwoman has done is to adopt the idea of the virtue, but forget the original reason for its existence, and it is ironical that the women who pride themselves on their housewifery today are those with the least economic need to deploy it.

It is true that in some areas of self-sufficiency economy still plays a large part. We have grown up in an egalitarian and inflation-ridden age, struggled through first jobs that paid a pittance which never even began to narrow the gap with the rising cost of living, and with every successive pay rise have found that, funnily enough, we never ended up any better off. Our standards of living have risen too, to match our income or outstrip it; we found that we had outgrown the enjoyment of bare floors and packing-case furniture; that a hamburger was no longer our idea of a meal out, nor spaghetti of a dinner-party dish in; that we were beginning to demand unlimited hot water, the use of a car or telephone, a television and reasonably expensive holidays as prerequisites rather than luxuries; that we wanted to buy our own homes; that children are an expensive indulgence. Small wonder then, if we don't feel we can afford to get the decorators in, when it's so easy to slap a coat of paint on ourselves, or to have the curtains made up when we already possess an expensive sewing machine. We have got into the habit of not being able to afford it, and our pride in our skill at achieving the task ourselves is at least partly based on the genuine concept of management as well as on the romantic one that Superwoman has instilled in us.

Actually, it is surprising what you can afford. You may well find it difficult to lay your hands on a spare couple of hundred pounds – most of us would retort tartly that a spare tenner would be just as unlikely – but it is worth considering just how much economy you actually do effect by doing it yourself. You tend to measure the decorator's estimate against an optimistic zero cost for your own efforts: yet paint and paper are more expensive for you to buy than for him to; you will also need to provide brushes, rollers, gallons of white spirit, and masking tape, and all the other incidentals which are already covered by his labour charge; then there is the extra expense you risk of paying to have paint spots removed from the carpet or your clothes, or buying more wallpaper because you stuck a length on upside down, or overpasted it so it disintegrated: and this is all without paying any heed to the theoretical cost of your time, or the annoyance factor of having the room uninhabitable for a fortnight, where a professional would leave it liveable-in even while the work was going on, and would have it finished in three days anyway. Certain mechanical repairs can also turn out to be false economies, unless you really know what you're doing (in which case I recommend opening a garage pretty smartly, the profits they make): I speak from bitter experience of having spent a whole day trying to replace a petrol pump ('It won't take ten minutes', he said) only to give up in the end and get a garage to do it: their total bill including a new pump came to two pounds more than the cost of the same pump to me, and I didn't get a perfectly good shirt ruined by oil-stains in the process: who in their right mind would begrudge two pounds to save a shirt and a day?

So you can see that a quick totting-up session might well be in order before you embark on a major refurbishment enterprise: even if you calculate that you'd still be saving twenty pounds, say, is it really worth it? And besides, money has a number of peculiar properties, one of which is the way that the pay rise never seems to materialize as extra income: equally, strangely enough, one-off expenditure that promises at the time to place you on the verge of bankruptcy has rarely, three months hence, made any significant difference to the normal state of your bank balance. What happens is that you automatically economize on everything else, sometimes without even noticing that you're doing so, and your affairs therefore gradually readjust themselves. It sounds incredibly naive, but (within reason, of course) it really does seem to be true: you won't grow rich by thinking that way, but if you do experiment, and find that it works, you'll gain a great deal in terms of peace of mind.

Quite apart from the financial considerations, have you really got the time to spare on adding yet another job to the thousands you already do, and will you really be happy to live with the results of your handiwork if you're sneakily aware of its imperfections? Your contentment, as you survey the gleaming vista of the finally completed dining-room, will be diminished by your exhausted relief that that's one chore done, or slightly marred by the knowledge that you've botched the edge of the window frame a bit, even if it doesn't show, or that the wallpaper beside the door is slightly misaligned, or that the carpet doesn't quite meet the skirting-board behind the sofa. And there is an anticlimactic effect with any decorating job, particularly, which takes more than a day to complete: the effect you've achieved may be everything you'd hoped, but it will be lessened for you because you know what it looked like half done, instead of gliding in one easy movement from vision to reality, like in the glossy magazine before-and-after pictures. And by the time you've lived, breathed and practically drowned in leaf green for a fortnight, you *hate* the wretched colour anyway.

And once you go beyond the paint-and-paper aspects of decorating to start on the wiring, the plumbing and the carpentry, your not-quite-professionalism really begins to tell. The frustrations of living with a wobbly kitchen counter or a slightly-out-of-true bookcase far outweigh for any woman the cost of having it done right in the first place (not so for most outmodedly conditioned men, whose delight in their own handiwork surpasses any niggles about whether the results are practical or not). Besides which, it's distinctly unSuperwomanly to turn up at a board meeting with your fingernails torn to shreds by splinters, and a blister the size of a shilling on your thumb, so if you will persist in being a fully-rounded human being then only the gentlest of carpentry is to be recommended. Wiring and plumbing should be left firmly to professionals on the grounds of safety: convince yourself that however carefully you followed the instructions you will never be completely sure that the whole electrical system isn't going to burst into flames at any minute, or that you haven't created a potentially dangerous airlock in the pipes when you plumbed in the washing machine. With your capacity for paranoia about your own inadequacy, it shouldn't be too difficult, and since you're paranoid anyway you might as well let it work for you. Which doesn't mean you can claim incompetence to change a fuse, a washer or a plug – there are limits to the value of ignorance, and these small chores are way on the far side of them – but it does mean, quite simply, that you recognize the point at which a professional is going to do his job better, faster, and perhaps even more cheaply, than you could ever hope to.

Part of the reason for breaking out into these happy pursuits is almost certainly your drive to prove that they are not the sole preserve of men. As with their offices and their sport, so with their DIY: there is still a large body of men who do like to create a mystique about the whole subject, laced with the arcane jargon of two-by-fours and chuck keys, and with a collection of wonderful toys as the badge of their membership of an exclusive (male) sect. Give him a Workmate, an electric drill with lots of spare bits, and a handful of chisels, screwdrivers and bright shiny nails, and he'll be as happy as with a model railway or a home computer: if you're very lucky, you may be admitted to his temple as an acolyte, and allowed to hold things steady, or measure up the next plank, or hand him tools while he engages in the serious business which you'd never understand. He will then be extremely cross when you say 'But I thought we were going to build it round the skirting board' or 'Shouldn't that diagonal be going the other way?' especially when you were, and it should; you will probably then be banished to the outer darknesses of the kitchen for challenging his authority while he redoes it all and hopes you won't know that that's what he's doing.

And though it's tempting to join in the game, by

refusing to understand anything about it, by insisting on calling a chisel 'that sharp blade thing' or denying any conceptual awareness of a rawlplug, you don't help to reduce DIY to more practical levels by doing so, but are rather leaving his way clear to build as many mystiques around it as he wants. If, on the other hand, you know what the tools are and what they can do, and persist in regarding them simply as tools, not virility symbols, you will quickly find that quite a lot of apparently impossibly complicated rituals are actually simple jobs which you can perfectly well tackle yourself without any fuss or bother as long as you have the physical strength to manage them. This discovery, however, isn't one you should parade unthinkingly before the world at large – if you can get away with having someone else to do them for you, why not just keep quiet and let him get on with it until you *need* to use your own ingenuity? That way he'll be happy, you'll have one less thing to worry or feel guiltily inadequate about, and you will still be secure in the knowledge that you can cope if you have to: which is after all what life is supposed to be about.

If men are jealous of their DIY, they're a hundred times more jealous of their cars. We all know the standard routine about sexual transference; the way all cars are 'she', yet also act as an extension of the driver's masculinity: we've all been bored out of our minds time and again by Sunday afternoons spent shivering by the roadside, contorted into impossible positions to hold sludgy black ends of things while some man tut-tuts excitedly over a fascinating mechanical problem, and by lunchtimes or evenings ignored in the corner of a bar full of enthusiastic talk of big ends and brake horse power. Women don't stand a chance against cars, nor in them either: 'woman driver' is both the worst insult a male motorist can hurl at another male motorist, and an indulgently contemptuous explanation for everything any woman ever suffers on wheels, from a gear mischange to the engine bursting into flames while she is unlucky enough to be in the driving seat. Women don't understand, far more than we don't understand carpentry or plumbing: how can a sex who believe that cars are convenient objects designed to get them easily from place to place ever *begin* to understand what cars really are? And the breed of men for whom cars are perks of the job are no better: sure, they don't spend their whole time under the bonnet (I knew one who took his into the garage to have the oil topped up) or waxing lyrical in lover-like terms they wouldn't think of using to you, but they do regard cars as symbols of power and so of virility in another way – slave concubine rather than capricious mistress, it's still a sex object not a means of transport.

Actually, of course, cars *are* machines designed for the convenience of our transport (and indeed a considerable safety factor for women at risk on foot), and with a minimum of regular attention they perform their function more than adequately. But they are machines designed by men for mechanics; an irritation, when they need emergency treatment, compounded by the fact that their nature requires them to be both dirty and physically difficult to operate on. It is all very well to limit your knowledge of what happens under the bonnet to replacing petrol, water, oil and brake fluid, and to apply to a garage for any further skills required, but there are times when the thing doesn't want to move and you need to make it – so you also need to know how to use jump leads on a dead battery, how to dry off spark plugs (or at least where they are, so you can point your proprietary spray can in roughly the right direction) and how to change a tyre. You then need to recognize the signs, when it is moving, of imminent collapse of the whole engine: it's easy enough to spot the little green light that says it wants oil, but how clued-up are you about the temperature and voltage meters, and do you know what to do if either starts vacillating alarmingly?

There is little or no excuse for avoiding this sort of

rudimentary knowledge: even if you have a company car, you don't have the right wantonly to worsen its ailments through sheer pig-headed ignorance, and if it's your own it can cost you a small fortune: with either, you still want to be able to use it *when* you want to. And it doesn't take a grandiose car maintenance class to teach you any of this – if you didn't already know it – just common sense and the manual, or a helpful friend to show you once, is enough: and unless you want to perpetuate the myth that women and cars are about as compatible as monkeys and word-processors or less so, you'd be well advised to learn immediately. But even if you do that, and even if you have made sure that the car is equipped with the necessary tools for dealing with normal emergencies, you should bear in mind that you are still at a disadvantage, and there will still be the infuriating times when however much of a Super-woman you are, you are impotently and furiously stuck either just because you're a woman or because you are so many other sorts of woman as well.

Changing a wheel, for instance, is theoretically a fairly straightforward business. You get the spare out of its hidey-hole in the boot and prop it up somewhere. You flip off the hubcap, whip out the wheelspanner and loosen the wheelnuts, then get out the jack, place it under the jacking point, and raise the car until there is no weight resting on the wheel to be removed. Then you undo the nuts until the wheel falls off: and then you put the new one in place and reverse the process . . . Like hell you do. You open the boot and find it's so full of the heavy junk left there from the last excursion under the bonnet, plus all the spares necessary for a three-month motoring holiday in Outer Mongolia, that you have to embark on a major removal job before you can even consider lifting the neat panel that covers the spare wheeel. The neat panel in question was designed to be lifted by a large meathook suspended directly above it and powered by several hundred kilo-watts, not by your finger and thumb from the only angle you can achieve without kneeling inside the boot on top of it. Underneath it are more spares, and roof-rack attachments and a can of 3-in-1 oil, placed inside the wheel to be out of the way; the 3-in-1 has leaked slightly, as you discover when you pause to mop your brow. A wheel is not only bulky, heavy and difficult to manoeuvre from a horizontal position over the lip of a boot; it is also tyred in rubber, which leaves large black marks all over the front of your clothes when you drag it forwards against yourself because that is the only way, not being a fifteen-stone muscle-bound rugby player, that you can get the leverage to lift it at all. Your hands, by the time you've rolled it to the pavement, are also black and feel greasy; this means you take longer than you might to assemble the jack, and transfer more grease to the jack and back to various parts of your person in the process. Putting the jack ready to one side, you are encouraged to discover that flipping off the hubcap is the work of a second, despite the fact that you've now knelt on the filthiest piece of road for fifty miles and ruined your skirt. So now you get out the wheel spanner, apply it to a nut, apply all your weight to it – and nothing happens. You try again. You try the other three nuts. The result remains absolutely the same: absolutely nothing. And at this point you suddenly realize the deep unfairness of it all: the fact that no amount of knowledge or expertise is going to be able to remove those nuts, but only brute force and ignorance; the fact that if they've been put on by some electronic fiend at the garage no man is going to be able to move them either; and the fact that you are nevertheless going to be derided as an incompetent female just for your lack of muscle. At this point, you frustratedly give up all thoughts of feminism and look for a man to bat your eyelashes at instead.

Even if you can cope with the physical requirements of a job, your ability to turn mechanic is still limited by circumstance. It may be a fairly easy task to check the spark plugs, but to dive under a bonnet in your cream linen suit on your way to meet your top American contact at the airport is out of the question. Women's shoes are not designed for jumping heavily on wheel spanners – I've broken a heel clean off trying – any more than light-coloured full skirts should be allowed even anywhere near a car door, never mind the bonnet. Superwoman, I have no doubt, keeps an old doctor's white coat and a pair of 'gardening shoes' or something equally acceptable in the car exactly for occasions like this, and a carton of those wipe clean things for her hands; but if you try it you'll almost inevitably find that you used the last one yesterday on a child's sticky fingers or a smudged eyelash, and the overall has been borrowed for dressing up, or is being washed, or hasn't been washed, so it'll make your clothes dirtier than the engine can. Once again, you have to swallow your principles and ask feebly for help – and grit you teeth against rude retorts to the varying degrees of kindly patronage that comes with it. And the most galling thing that ever happened to me was when I was quite happily tinkering away at a job I could do, until I had to enlist a passer-by to loosen a stubborn nut for me: he then kindly explained exactly what I was doing wrong (without prior knowledge of the idiosyncrasies of my car: I was doing it right). His generous offer to take over for me, still in his city suit, was not, I'm afraid, received with proper gratitude . . .

Whether under the bonnet or behind the wheel, you simply have to accept that you're on to a loser: nothing you do will be right anyway, so your best bet is to concentrate on regular maintenance and servicing to ensure that as far as possible you don't have to do anything. And for the wheel-changing problem there is now an answer: a pressurized canister of rubber solution which you simply attach to the valve and which then seals the puncture from within – even in a cream linen suit you can manage that.

Both DIY and car maintenance are important skills to would-be Superwomen in that they are proof of competence in a traditionally male field and therefore appeal to your feminist principles. But the activities which receive infinitely more coverage and higher Brownie points are very definitely of the female, homemaking type: the feminist in Superwoman doesn't stand a chance against the Earth Mother. Knitting, for example, is such a sine qua non that it hardly need be mentioned, except in terms of an occasional exciting new pattern, or ideas for new-look yarns to knit with: Superwoman was apparently born with needles clicking in her ears, and even if she never becomes a Patricia Roberts, her homemade sweaters can be worn in public with pride. She is also assumed to sew, at least to a fairly basic level of cotton skirts, cushions and curtains, but preferably with a capacity for designing and running up her own elegant outfits and petit-pointing exquisitely accurate chair covers as well. You shun these skills at your peril, for although men probably don't know that they're a vital contribution to the quality of life, and care less, other women who do possess them will despise you for being either feebly defeatist or for denying your femininity or both unless you display some sort of competence as a couturier. (I have never understood this: I spent three terms of needlework classes making the apron we were supposed to run up in the first week, and though many have tried long and hard to teach me to knit even one row of plain, none ever succeeded, whereas I can drive a car or wield a screwdriver with reasonable competence.) A car engine, or the bits of it you can be expected to deal with, seems childishly simple by comparison with a sewing machine; wood and nails infinitely easier to match compatibly than different weights or tensions of cloth and yarn; accurate draughtmanship more vital in dressmaking than in carpentry (since you can't cover up your errors with plastic wood and a coat of paint); and one smudgy fingermark or misplaced pin can render the end result less than acceptable. It is ridiculous to believe that because hemming and button replacement is easy all sewing is, but that *is* the vague general belief, encouraged by the tradition of its being woman's work and therefore necessarily kindergarten stuff, beneath the contempt of men except at the very highest level of couture. The unworthy suspicion that for 'beneath the contempt' you might accurately read 'beyond the capability' – have you ever watched an untutored man sewing on a button? – only highlights the con trick involved in making women feel inadequate if they can't do it either . . .

Admitting an inability to sew or knit can be an enormous relief. You can buy the clothes you want to, without feeling honour – bound to calculate how much cheaper it would be to make up an approximation to them yourself; you are freed from the oppression of life with not quite perfectly gathered curtains, or ones with the pins still in the hem four years after you hung them; you can sit and read, or watch television, or talk, without a puritanical urge to occupy your idle hands like a tricoteuse in the front row at the guillotine; you can preserve Joanna's latest from at least one fiddly, difficult-to-launder matinée jacket or smocked dress and give it something much more acceptable like building bricks instead. Nor do you have to forego the pleasure of home-made: mothers and mothers-in-law, feeling inadequate themselves in the face of your all-round competence and freedom, are often delighted to be able to offer you something for Christmas and birthday presents that you really want and can't provide better yourself; if you're lucky enough to know a struggling young designer (and there are lots about) you can enjoy the luxury of couture clothes or professional household draperies at a fraction of the price of the upper end of the ready-made market, and in the happy knowledge that you're providing employment and much-needed cash to a burgeoning young talent – thereby promoting the somewhat confused Superwoman ideal of a society keeping alive the traditional crafts much more effectively than if you put them all out of business by doing it yourself.

Again, of course, this doesn't mean that you should announce with defiant pride your total inability to thread a needle or achieve a straightforward hemming stitch, any more than you can pretend to exist in sublime ignorance of the function of a car battery or the wiring of a standard three-point plug. It also doesn't mean that if you enjoy dressmaking or knitting you should give it up as a matter of principle and take to twiddling your thumbs miserably instead. But Mistress of the Wardrobe is a separate position from Housekeeper and Company Director and Nanny: you don't have to take it on unless you want to. Your femininity will survive the lack of a dressmaking diploma or a black belt in knitting; your self-confidence won't survive any further accusations of inadequacy you can find to throw at yourself.

Even more unnatural than needlecraft as a 'basic' womanly skill is upholstery. The type of work involved in this appears completely incompatible with the ordered elegance of Superwoman's lifestyle: nail-breaking, muscle-binding, hand-bruising, lung-searing labour goes into all those neat button-back chairs and outwardly velvet-smooth sofas, which hide beneath their poised exteriors a seething morass of horsehair stuffing, chunks of splintery wood and viciously strong webbing. Moreover, the range of tools needed for the job is various, expensive, fairly difficult to come by and painful to use, and does seem to represent quite a high investment in the trade – because upholstery is not something you can tackle with the odds and ends of equipment you have to hand. The fascination in it obviously comes from the contrast between messy innards and elegant exteriors, and most people enjoy sheer hard labour once in a while – but there can certainly be no grounds for self-castigation if you are reluctant to tackle it: that would be like feeling guilty and parasitic because you don't make your own shoes, which involves much the same sort of specialist tools and craft processes. And since upholstery is one of the range of crafts whose passing from the commercial world is most often lamented, surely it is one that you should be nurturing, rather than helping to kill it by arrogating it to your own sphere? After all, in your capacity as Organization Woman you make a point of knowing and using small businesses (your 'little men') and you will only get more neurotic and schizophrenic than ever if you persist in facing yourself with too many contradictions like that.

Whatever she may get up to elsewhere, Superwoman's extra-mural skills really come into full force in the kitchen. Just as the epitome of her public face is as hostess of the dinner party, so her inner Superwomanhood is epitomized by her talent for feeding people as well. The plum sorbet and the tender young French beans she gives her dinner guests are fresh from her own garden via the freezer, but they are only the tip of an iceberg of subsidiary succulence in her groaning larder. Superwoman doesn't only cook for the dinner party of the moment; she's cooking for the survival of the species, and the fruits of her labour would do justice to the kitchens of a substantial self-sufficient castle. If she were forced to use her larder as a fall-out shelter she would not only survive, but thrive and grow plump, such is her Earth Mother obsession with abundance in harvesting and generosity in nourishing her brood. From sloe gins, to lemon marmalades and a range of jams, jellies and chutneys you will never see in any shop, to pickled cucumbers or hoards of fruit cake and spice biscuits, she diligently squirrels away, gathering and gleaning, boiling and baking, obsessively feeding her freezer and larding her larder with delicious plenty, all neatly labelled and dated and stored in suitable quantities for small or medium-sized gifts as well as for family consumption. This one attribute, her providence, seems to override all others in the ethos of her womanhood; the primeval maternal urge to feed the brutes to answer every other challenge to her excellence in any other field; and your guilt, if you fail to live up to her exacting standards of provision, is commensurately the greater.

Now baking and preserving are all very well when it's a matter of creating delicious foods you can't otherwise get or which are completely inferior when emanating from a supermarket shelf to the genuine home-made article.

Fresh-baked bread and cakes and biscuits *do* taste much nicer than the commercial sort, and *are* healthier as well – but it would be healthier still not to eat them at all, and a peckish five-year-old will find even sliced white ambrosial. Children (and most men) are extraordinarily ungrateful and materialistic beasts, who would much rather eat Mr Kipling's cakes than yours, and regard the purchase of crisps and Wonderloaf as far more evidential of the abundance of your love than the conscientious provision of any amount of warm-from-the-oven wholemeal or savoury biscuits from historical recipes, so if you have kidded yourself you're baking and boiling on their account, you can forget it: you're either doing it for yourself or you're doing it to compete with Superwoman. There is justifiable pride in eating the result of your own labours, whether it's a devil's food cake or young vegetables from the garden, and even if the improvement in their flavour weren't discernible to the average jaded palate, you would still be right to assume that it is enhanced by the work that has gone into it and by the element of genuine wonder at the combined creativity of yourself and nature. And natural providence does rather rebel at letting the fruits scattered liberally – if uncommercially – all over the countryside fall to the birds' portion or rot on their stems, when you can browse on them at will and reap the dual benefits of almost free, otherwise unavailable food and the admiring plaudits of your peers. It would be a shame never to taste rowan or quince or crab-apple jelly, for instance, when the undeniably hard labour that goes into their production is so amply justified by the taste, and the same goes for sloe gin, or elderflower wine, or even fresh blackberries, which appear so briefly and expensively in the greengrocer's shop, but so abundantly on the disused railway cutting. But it is easy to forget to ask yourself whether you actually want these things, or whether you simply assume you must want them because they're there, or because the latest cookery book or glossy magazine has extolled their virtues to you. Without a certain amount of watchful caution you can find yourself so blinded by the necessity of your providence for its own sake that you completely lose track of the usefulness or desirability of the end result: following an age-old instinct to preserve and make appetising what food is available, you forget that you no longer have an imperative to hoard against winter starvation or a restricted diet for long periods of the year. Food that is preserved to prevent it being wasted *is* wasted, and it wastes your time and effort as well.

The most conspicuous parable for carrying a good idea too far is tomato chutney, which suddenly appeared a few years ago as an ubiquitous measure of Superwomanhood. You were a complete failure if you didn't have a larder full of it; whole conversations narrowed to a comparison of weights and measures, and the availability or otherwise of suitable receptacles. Tomato chutney is in fact a perfect parallel for the self – fulfilling futility of the pursuit of the Superwoman myth; a proof of perpetual motion that would boggle the minds of the romantic searchers after that phenomenon; a true example, when carried beyond the limits of common sense, of the end being completely obscured by the means, the results bearing no relation to the labour. It is an Awful Warning to any Trap-ee, and it goes something like this:

First you grow your tomatoes, potting them tenderly, watering them daily, and anxiously measuring their progress by half-inches. When you go on holiday you have to leave a key and strict instructions with a neighbour or friend to rear your delicate offspring as they would their own (I know you do: I've been caught four times). You take weaklings into the office or your bedroom, where they sit inconveniently on the windowsill to drink up all the sun you can offer them; you wage war on aphids. You cluck over your little crop like a broody hen. Despite the fact that tomatoes are quite absurdly easy to grow, you are overcome with delight when your efforts are rewarded by small green nodules popping up all over the plants: just like half the population, you have successfully grown tomatoes!

You pick them, counting and weighing each one as if it were a diamond, when they are plump and green, and lay them in trays to redden in the sun. Every windowsill in the house begins to look like a greengrocer's stall at four-thirty on a Saturday, with its forlorn row of half a dozen semi-blushing fruits. You turn them daily. You pick and count and weigh more. The windowsills are filling up. Tomatoes in the shops are down to 12p a pound. The 'shopping list' column of your newspaper starts talking about gluts and giving recipes for iced tomato soup. You make iced tomato soup, which tastes remarkably of iced tomatoes. You make ratatouille, which tastes largely of tomatoes as well. You have tomato salads and grilled tomatoes with every meal. You painstakingly scald their skins off and use them in place of the much more delicious tinned plum tomatoes in your cooking. You give them away by the bagful to less provident friends and relations. Stallholders start giving them away with lettuces. You discover that when it comes down to it, there isn't an awful lot you can do with a tomato. But your windowsills remain bizarrely decorated with rows of pustulous sub-Christmas tree ornaments. You are beginning to become desperate at the very though of tomatoes . . .

So you make tomato chutney. You beg, borrow and buy jars. You lay in, at vast expense, pounds and pounds of sugar and apples or onions, and gallons of white vinegar. You spend hours weighing and counting all over again, then more hours scalding and skinning, seething and stirring. You strain it. You strain yourself and the household. You fill every pan in the house and immobilize the cooker. You cool the chutney. It is neither red nor green, but an indeterminate brown. You ladle it into jars, seal them and label them. You taste it. It occurs to you that there is nothing particularly special about tomato chutney. You give it to your family or friends: from the silence, you deduce that they don't think it's particularly special either.

You press jars of it on every visitor, trying to avoid their eyes as they wanly search for some suitably grateful response. You clean out the larder and proudly store it there in military ranks of gleaming productivity. It stays there, in permanent testament to your housewifery: nearly two years' supply of tomato chutney, which nobody ever wanted, which has probably cost you far more in financial terms, from Gro-bag to jar, than it would have had you voluntarily bought the stuff in the same quantities, and which has certainly cost you far more in totally purposeless effort. And the real tragedy of this sad little story is that next year you'll plant your tomato plants with exactly the same optimism as you did this . . .

Put like that, of course, it's not tragic at all, but very funny – if it happens to somebody else. And yet it can so easily happen to you, or me, or any of us, and does all the time: not necessarily with tomato chutney, nor windfall apples (another fertile area for perpetual motion), nor even expensive experiments in silk, or wood, or petrol pumps, but in any and every area of our activities where we let the chore take over insensibly from the pleasure, the labour from the hire. At least in the field of your extra-mural pursuits it is easier to see, than in anything more basic like your career or your housework, just how much unnecessary labour you could be avoiding. You can appreciate the possibility of paying somebody else to do what is their job, rather than doing it yourself, whose it isn't; or of the job in question being a frill which might be nice but is certainly dispensable. So ask yourself, before you embark on any of these perilous enterprises, whether you really have the time and inclination or only a sense of obligation to take them on at all. Consider whether bramble jelly is more vital to your well-being than *Brookside*. If time is money, are you saving enough for luxuries? If pottering around among the jelly pans or up to your knees in horsehair is still your idea of a good time, good luck to you. But if it bores you rigid, or makes you feel faint to think about it, or it consumes you with horror to conceive of the work you're letting yourself in for, remember the tomato chutney and pause. Outside the armed forces and the more eccentric religious sects, no duty is supposed to be performed for its own sake; there is always a choice. Like, don't.

# 11
## *Sisters*

Superwoman doesn't have much truck with feminism, despite having assimilated so many of the movement's principles with her own. She can't help feeling that it's undignified, unfeminine and rather childish to rant against injustice instead of just getting on and running the place (and thereby proving her case by example instead of attacking the opposite one), and that it does more to diminish the status of women than to augment it. She doesn't really like to be seen to hold strong 'political' views, since that would make it difficult for her to be all things to all women; besides, she is proud of her appearance and doesn't see why she shouldn't make the most of it instead of looking plain and unmade-up, as she imagines feminists have to. Moreover, Superwoman is already confident of her right and her ability to take her equal place in a man's world, without ever having shed her belief in the importance of her traditional feminine role as helpmeet as well: in general, she is pretty firmly convinced of the overall superiority of her sex, so that any move towards equality could only be for her a retrograde step. She doesn't argue against the champions of liberation, though she may occasionally chide them for 'going too far' – in fact she joins whole-heartedly in condemning lenient rape sentences; campaigns for, and takes full advantage of, equal pay, improved maternity benefits and nursing facilities in public lavatories; mildly deplores the current trend towards early marriages and the imbalance of unemployment to the detriment of women; and will castigate roundly the hapless waiter who presents the wine list or bill to her male lunch guest. At heart, however, she isn't really at ease with theories which are not only uncompromisingly definite and potentially political, but which also conflict so basically with her deep-rooted instincts to mate, to nest-build and to nourish. To cover her uncertainty she does her best to ignore them, which frustrates the radical feminists enormously, because having so much influence with the rank and file Superwoman would be a valuable addition to their numbers, and like everyone else with a cause they are baffled by the spectacle of an influential figure who is neither for them nor against them.

But if you think this antipathy to feminism does anything to make Superwoman more sympathetic towards her unradical, merely feeble, sisters, you are wrong. She heaps blistering scorn – or worse, patient encouragement – on those too diffident, too indifferent or too otherwise occupied to fight tooth and nail for the managing directorship; she briskly annihilates protestations of inefficiency in any field from rally-cross to raffia work; she has no sympathy at all, as she will firmly tell you, with emotional problems, errors of judgement or illness, all of which she assumes the sufferer to have brought upon herself; she is impatient with anything less than perfection in dress or in organization, and anything less than a computer-like brain and a rapier-like speed of answer; she is amusedly horrified if you admit you can't make pastry ('But it's so *easy*!'), and callously brutal with any shortfall in your self-assertion. She drives other women as hard as she drives herself – if not harder, on the grounds that we have so much further to go: underneath her civilized exterior, she really believes that the race is to the swift and the battle to the strong (*pace* Ecclesiastes,) and that only weeds are found by the wayside.

Which leaves you, as neither a Superwoman nor a single-minded feminist, in a no-win situation, because without being one or other of them you're open to attack by both, unless you opt out completely and let all insults and exhortations alike sail harmlessly over your carefully lowered head. But to be really safely out of the firing line you would have to miss out on the things you do want to master as well as those you can't don't care about: you decide to compete only in your chosen events because Superwoman, once she's got a toe-hold in your conscience, doesn't need any further invitation to trample all over it; and to abandon your career ambitions along with your tyre- changing skills because you can't be perfect at both would be petulantly defeatist and a bit like cutting off your nose to spite your face. Anyway, if there is by some remote chance any point on which Superwoman can't fault you, I have no doubt that Radical Feminist will be able to, which may be hard luck but is the way it is at the moment, so you might as well accept it straight away to avoid disappointment.

In any case, you *do* want to compete – you wouldn't be in the Superwoman Trap if you didn't – and being a normally perverse sort of person you want to compete both on behalf of, but most of all against, other women. This is, of course, all the fault of men, though the poor things probably don't know it. Even if they recognize and accept their share of the blame for the inequality of the sexes, and so for your laudable urge to fight a war on behalf of women, they won't realize that your instinct to outdo other women can be laid at their door as well: it is usually of academic interest to the prize who's going to win it. Yet long before Superwoman appeared on the scene we'd been at each other's throats for centuries, spitting and snarling over men: since the chief success open to us was to catch one, and (at least in a monogamous society) the rule was one each and no sharing, then of course all other women were our rivals; especially as there weren't usually quite enough to go round, and of the ones there were some could spoil the odds even more by acceptably staying single, which women, of course, couldn't. When Superwoman stepped in to extend the range of our ambitions, our rivalry with our sisters came along for the ride and transferred itself to all our other fields of competition, while the men, whose fault it all is, carry on more or less unmolested. Thus even fighting our way up the careers ladder we are more likely to blame our female colleagues than our male ones for placing rubs in the way, whether by being too stridently contentious or too submissively contented; we instinctively want to outdo Nicola in the boardroom and Sally in bed, and once you enter the domestic arena of comparative cookery or competitive childcare, then the gloves are really off with a vengeance. As in all families, we reserve the full fury of our sibling rivalry for siblings of the same sex (and at the same time need their approval the more); Superwoman, naturally, trades on this deeply unpleasant but only human trait in us, and uses it against us with a marked degree of success.

Perhaps we also mind less about losing out to a man because we can blame social history: we may resent it, but we don't have to look any further for the cause of our failure than the one biological error of being born the wrong sex, which was hardly our fault. Other women, however, are starting under the same handicaps as ourselves, and are therefore in fair competition, so that if we lose out to one of them we can't dismiss our inadequacy as the mere fabrication of a prejudiced world. And we're regrettably quick to come up with reasons to account for her success and compensate for our incipient complex: how many times have you listened – or, shame on you, subscribed – to the excuse that she only got the job because the managing director fancied her; or of course she can cook like an angel, when she can afford all the best ingredients and spent a year at Cordon Bleu school (while you were doing something worthy and under-privileged like hitching to Katmandu); or her taste is very smart, but terribly suburban and conventional? And even if we're feeling generous enough to allow her one area of superiority, we'll counter it with a comforting complementary failure – of course she has to throw herself into her work, as you happen to know her love life's a disaster; with looks like that, you suppose she doesn't need a brain as well; how a nice, sensible girl like that can waste herself on that archetypal male chauvinist, you'll never know. When we compare woman to woman, like to like, we measure every facet of them against our own insecurities, which doesn't leave much scope for charity or even justice in our judgements. It is all very reprehensible, and not at all what you'd expect from the so-called gentle sex, especially when we're meant to be supporting each other in total solidarity against men; more to the point, it allows Superwoman to play us off gleefully against one another, and so keep us firmly trapped, which is far more harmful than the bickering itself.

But on the other side of the coin is the strong sense of loyalty we feel for our own sex against attack from outside (in other words, men again); like a family, we close ranks against any threat to one of our number by someone not of our number. When Juliet complains that Roger's being a swine, you don't hesitate to join her sympathetically in reviling him; you lie unblinkingly on your friends' behalf about their whereabouts, unquestioningly take their part over their extravagances, their follies and their downright misbehaviour, in exactly the same way as men cover up for each other in the face of a monstrous regiment of women. You genuinely do feel a crusading urge to fight every inch of the way up your career structure for the sake of your younger sisters as well as yourself – even while you're resenting the fact, as elder sisters will, that you do the work and they reap the benefit of it; by the same token, you support them at least tacitly in their crusades, however wrongheaded they may seem to you. Why you should behave in this altruistic fashion to your sisters, at the same time as competing vigorously against them, is a mystery, and the only answer to it is that you are part of the great conspiracy of the sexes, which is as old as the human race and not a new invention of the feminist movement at all. Women command your complicity and you theirs simply because you *are* women, and women have helped each other out in childbirth, in harvest time, in widowhood, in famine and in every other crisis that came along since we first grunted at each other from cave to cave, not just since we started setting up women's community centres in Penge. This loyalty is no more thoroughly explicable than is our rivalry, but the end result is that we do feel we have a duty to blaze the trail; our feminist principles, however far we carry them, are based on something more complex and more permanent than mere intellectualization or the convenient co-operation of comrades-at-arms, and so we wholeheartedly campaign against injustices that don't affect us personally, comply with feminist arguments we don't agree with, connive at seduction scenes with which we are at equal ideological loggerheads, and take comfort and enjoyment from the sexual solidarity of 'girls' talk'. When she isn't being our natural rival our sister is our natural ally, and we therefore don't question her motives any more that she would ours: in the last resort, we both know we can rely on complete mutual support. And Superwoman, once more, knows it too, and uses it as a lever to manipulate us further into her Trap.

It's no wonder if you're confused – and it certainly seems particularly hard that your problems with the Trap should be so thoroughly exacerbated by the attitudes of women to other women when you had, surely, the right to expect that being all in the same boat you might all be heading in roughly the same direction. But if you were blithely imagining that, you were forgetting that the Superwoman myth was, after all, created not only *for* women, but *by* women, and since Hell hath no fury like a Superwoman scorned it is among other women that you will always encounter the most resistance to your attempts to get out of her clutches.

Men, after all, have no reason to care very much whether you're a Superwoman or not; life is equally peaceful or equally complicated for them either way, and it really doesn't make much difference whether you're saving them from making decisions or forcing them to compete, or vice versa. But we don't really mind what they think, because they're only boys; we do care very much, on the other hand, what the girls think. You mustn't forget that a whole generation and more of women have put an awful lot of work into creating Superwoman and spreading her word; that we did badly need her image to bolster up our self-confidence and so equip us for the early battles for equality as it is lived, rather than as a paper ideal: so it's not really surprising that large numbers of us are still fiercely fighting the revolution on her behalf long after she's stopped being a revolutionary. And that's really the problem: indoctrinate enough of the female sex with the ideal of Superwoman, and we go on to preach it and enforce it among the rest; any of us thinking of backsliding then has to cope with the dual traumas first of convincing ourselves that we had gone too far, and then avoiding being spurred on to greater efforts by other women. It's a vicious circle, and an extraordinarily difficult one to break out of: even if you do firmly quieten that voice in your head which tells you Superwoman is right, you run a fairly high risk of being accused of feeble cowardice by your media gurus and alternately being bullied, cajoled and shamed back into line by your similarly trapped female peers. It's a notable feature of the Superwoman Trap that the more people there are in it, the more difficult it is for any one of them to get out.

It can be hard to explain to a dedicated follower of excellence on all fronts that you don't particularly like making watercress soup, though you still enjoy sewing; or that you're indifferent to what happens under the car bonnet as long as something does, yet are nevertheless ambitious for your career – they may seem like separate issues to any normal person, but they aren't to Superwoman (and therefore not to you either, in your more would-be moods). In Superwoman's book, even one negative on your rating card can all too frequently cancel out any number of pluses, so until you pull your socks up in your weak subjects you won't get any credit for your strong ones. And all the time, your fellow Trap-ees will continue to jolly you along, both by example and advice, towards success across the board: your backsliding – or even simply not sliding forward far and fast enough – is a collective failure for the whole Superwoman ethos; a letting-the-side-down sort of general disappointment, and one that could threaten the whole enterprise to boot. Every woman you've ever met therefore has a right to offer helpful criticism in the hope of setting you back on the right course – just as (if you're a would-be Superwoman and honest with yourself, you'll have to admit) you do the same for them.

So argue that you've followed Superwoman's lead for long enough, and now you can make it on your own: your sisters will speak to you more in sorrow than in anger of self-delusion, or the easy way out, or not giving up now when you're so nearly there (wherever 'there' is), or sternly of the example that you, as one of the lucky vanguard, are duty bound to show the rank and file behind. Complain that you thought Superwoman offered the promise of freedom, not a military dictatorship, and they will chide you for your selfishness in riding with the cause only for your own ignoble ends, or for your impatience in expecting the battle to be so easily won. Question the attainability of the Superwoman ideal itself, if you dare; you will only confirm their belief that you're chickening out, and they can, moreover, point triumphantly to any one of a dozen or so paragons among your acquaintance or the latest crop of magazines to prove you conclusively wrong.

This is where they've really got you (or you've got them), because example is by far the strongest weapon we have in order to keep every other woman just as trapped as ourselves, being easily the most effective counter-argument against wishy-washy revisionism (which is also, of course, why we have to keep reassuring our fragile egos by bitching, so lamentably unconvincingly even to ourselves, about the women who outdo us). No properly brought-up Trap-ee can really believe in her heart that anyone else can do something she can't. So in vain do you protest that you're perfectly self-confident without the managing directorship, when Gloria's going round like a cat with the cream because she's got hers; how can you deny that you want a model figure, when it's the slimming season, and every paper or magazine you open is urging you to new ways of giving yourself one on the assumption that you do; or claim you're happy without much idea of how to boil an egg when Louise's haute cuisine makes you feel so guiltily envious? And there is always some real all-round Superwoman acolyte out in magazine-land, beaming at you in glorious technicolour from her spotless but homely kitchen on a double-page spread just after the health section, surrounded by an adoring family and an array of tempting dishes she's just about to offer them: the text tells you she successfully combines her demanding career with helping her husband set up his embryonic but exciting new business, bringing up their four children, and running a water-polo class for underprivileged grandmothers, and has renovated their charming Tudor farmhouse single-handed; in the pictures she looks as if she'd just strayed in from the fashion pages – clothes designed and hair styled, naturally, by herself. No matter how much our reason tells us that she can't possibly be the norm, no matter how avidly we read between the lines for proof that this superlative Sandra from Suffolk is really an out-and-out bitch and very boring as well – as long as she's there, we will always find it difficult to regard Superwoman completely as a myth: as long as there's someone with a face and a name to compete with, the race is still on.

The sensible solution to this problem of feminine peer-group pressure and comparative achievement is to start up a rearguard action among your similarly rebellious peers. There are enough of you, sitting moping in your winebars and over your kitchen tables bemoaning your lot, to develop a small but effective task force capable of convincing yourselves out of the Trap rather than into it. After all, it's a fair bet that the women you like enough to be moping in winebars with are the ones whose opinions you care about most anyway, and if they're moping with you then presumably they'd like to get out of the trap too. Even though you'll still need to hold your own against the rest of the world, the knowledge that your *real* friends agree with you will do wonders for your mutinous tendencies. So if, instead of encouraging each other to bewail your inadequacy and your general overworkedness, and indulge your guilt complexes, you egged each other on to go out and find a home-help; if, rather than complaining hopelessly that you never seem to do anything for yourself any more, you were to arrange a joint day out in Brighton or even a late-night shopping spree, you might end up gradually subverting more would-be Superwomen than you could guess: the power of example works both ways. (And this book was born in a winebar moan . . . )

Alternatively, in view of Superwoman's distrust for feminism, you might persuade her to leave you in peace by claiming you'd abandoned her cause for the cause of radical liberation: one extremist tends to recognize the futility of wasting her ammunition on another. Unfortunately, however, one extreme is just as unattractive as the other, and since Superwoman and Radical Feminist are sisters under the skin you might also have some difficulty in recognizing which is which. The transfer of ideals and party lines from one to the other is bewilderingly rapid, and quite often they both share the same ones at the same time: Superwoman is as likely to accuse you of feebleness for not being intimately familiar with your clutch cable, and a hard line feminist to cry treachery to your sex if you deny the essential expression of your womanhood through childbirth, as vice versa; both or neither might just as easily celebrate your domesticity as deride your attachment to your middle-management job, or the other way round. The situation is further confused because, unlike Superwoman, you don't have neat partitions in your head to keep your ideas conveniently segregated and, unlike Radical Feminist, you haven't suborned them all to one single burning ideal: you probably half agree with both of them half the time, which makes their crossfire about as helpful and as comprehensible to you as a South American coup is to the average citizen. They both told you, and you foolishly believed them, that their sole aim was to liberate you and widen your options, so you might be forgiven for wondering why they are so often at loggerheads, and why between them the only option they often seem to have left you is to be wrong.

However faint-hearted you are about it, it's unlikely that you'll be able to maintain Superwoman's lofty approach to feminism, since its basic principles are so obviously unexceptionable and worthy of your support. Of course there are social inequalities to be equalled, wrongs to be righted, and reforms to be made; and of course Radical Feminist, like Superwoman, has done sterling work in bringing you as far as you've come towards an ideal world, so you will be lucky not to feel guilty if you don't support her wholeheartedly. But the strength of her ideal does sometimes lead her into preaching an awful lot of nonsense, and like Superwoman she tends to adopt an irritating nanny-knows-best tone with you, imposing strict rules on you for your own good impervious to any suggestion that you might by now have reached the age of reason and be entitled to bend them a little, or even make up a few of your own: she sometimes gets so intent on her skirmishes that she fails to see that the main battle has moved on beyond them, and might even have progressed far enough in our favour for us to temper our valour with discretion, and stop shooting cowards and prisoners.

Which is a pity, because her excess of zeal only serves to alienate the moderate majority from her legitimate causes along with her wilder vagaries, to retire with relief to the compromise position of the faint-hearted feminist, which allows us a welcome respite from eternal vigilance, and some latitude for inconsistency in occasionally indulging our reactionary tendencies to behave like sex (or preferably sexy) objects, or succumb to similar unsound ideologies without having to justify them on any more momentous grounds than that we *are* faint-hearted. Not many women enjoy feeling unkempt because they haven't shaved their legs or mascara-ed their eyelashes, or guilty because they have; most like the company of men as well as other women, but get tired of keeping their ears pinned back ready to react to every possible sign of sexism in the normal banter of social intercourse. It's hard to believe that *Winnie the Pooh* is really sexist just because Kanga is an archetypal mother figure, any more than Shakespeare was for writing all his female parts for boy players: it's also hard to believe that every minor lapse is going to make a major difference to the real issues at stake. Faint-hearted feminists don't particularly want to go on slaving away at the revolutionary imperatives of career, motherhood, car maintenance and multiple orgasms without some time off for rest and recreation, and after all, why should they?

Even if we are still some way from equality in the conservatively structured areas of employment and taxation, to name but two, or the more strongly sexually conditioned realms of domesticity and motherhood, we *have* reached the age of reason, and we have come far enough to relax a little, particularly in our social relationships. It is not only off-putting, but also pointless, for Radical Feminist to place a total ban on fraternizing with the enemy: no advantage can be gained by isolating women from the rest of the human race, withdrawing behind barriers as divisive as ever they were when built by a male-dominated society; you can't convert anyone if you don't talk to them; and sitting behind a self-erected fence nursing your grievances, however legitimate, doesn't do anything to redress them, or you any good. So you shouldn't feel guilty if you haven't been showing total solidarity with the besieged hardliners; it really does make more sense to follow your own muddled inclinations than to go into purdah, and if you do occasionally err on the side of generosity it's better than having to keep a jealous guard on your good nature all the time. And though this may sound a flippant thing to say, I don't know a single genuinely radical feminist who could honestly be called happy – which was surely largely the point?

The stock response to that, from a would-be feminist Superwoman, would no doubt be that yes, it is the point, but for the whole of womankind rather than for any one selfish individual, and while you're crusading against oppression it would be frivolous and futile to expect personal happiness – or even, heaven forbid, a little humour – before the battle is won. Even the normally non-feminist Superwoman follows the same puritanical ethic in exhorting her reluctant followers to put their duty before their immediate gratification, and once you add your own altruistic ideas of responsibility to the greater collective good to the mixture it gets pretty potent, and can quite easily seduce you back into the Trap with barely a murmur of protest; especially since the greater collective good in question is an improvement in the lot of women.

But before you convince yourself all over again that both Superwoman and Radical Feminists are therefore absolutely right to be urging you on to greater efforts on behalf of womankind, you might stop to consider that there's something very odd about their definition of the term. It always seems to refer to *other* women. The word, on the lips of this unholy pair, takes on a completely different meaning from the OED's 'adult female human beings', and apparently describes instead a nebulous collective entity, whose composition is both catholic and variable but which *never includes you*. It can't do, or your greater good would be part of the bargain as well, which it never appears to be. This is all very peculiar, and raises all sorts of interesting questions quite apart from your putative benefits from the greater collective good: like, if you can't be a woman – which you obviously can't, since your duty to women is clearly meant to apply to a repressed minority and not to yourself – then what are you? How can you describe your age and gender without misrepresenting yourself? Perhaps the minute you step outside whatever defines 'women' you become an honorary, or more likely dishonorary, man; or perhaps 'recidivist' will become the new word for 'average non-activist adult female human being'; or perhaps you're not a human being at all? Come to that, what are Superwoman and Radical Feminist, with their duty to 'women'? Are other women also not women with regard to their own advantage? And if you're not a woman, then why on earth are you worrying about your collective responsibility to your sisters, or indeed in the Superwoman Trap at all?

This is, of course, nonsense, but nonsense with a grain of truth in it. We do tend to forget the individual in our enthusiasm for the cause, which is laudable but not if carried to excess, and I'm sure you've heard just as often as I have that 'women need' or 'women want' or 'women think' something that you've never felt the remotest necessity or desire or interest for at all. But, despite the alarming usurpation of your identity, you are still one of the women for whom both Superwoman and Radical Feminist promised a better world, and you are therefore entitled to reap your own share of the harvest you helped to sow. Their original aim really *was* to give you the right to do exactly what you want to, without being oppressed by either of them any more than by men, and if they seem sometimes to have lost sight of that little detail, there's no reason for you to follow them blindly into slavery – a tyrant is still a tyrant, whatever its sex. All you need to do is have a quick confidence-boosting conference with your fellow winebar mutineers, take a deep breath, and tell them what you told men all those years ago – that your promised new freedom is there for the taking, and you're about to take it. Throw away their rule books, and after the first panic moment of insecurity you'll be astonished to find how far you'd already progressed beyond them.

Easier said than done? Well, yes, inevitably. But if you're still nagged by guilt at the thought of betraying your sisters, try to encompass one idea that Superwoman has signally failed to tell you about: since feminism means that every woman has the right to make her own choices without fear or favour, somebody has to put that into practice before any amount of ideological campaigning to prepare the ground will have an atom of effect. And so you'd actually be helping the cause enormously if you volunteered to be that pioneering somebody . . .

# 12
# *The Human Factor*

If you've got this far without collapsing from exhaustion, you will probably have come to the gradual unwelcome conclusion that you'll never make a Superwoman – which is absolutely true. You won't, and nor will any other woman, ever achieve the perfection of an ideal that doesn't and can't exist. On the other hand, a quick mental review of just what you already have achieved, in combining so many of her talents, attributes and existences within the framework of one real live human being, will justify you in realizing that you're actually rather more than a Superwoman – not only because you've managed to do so, but because you've left room for some vestiges of sanity, individuality and humour at the same time. In which case, you will see at once that any further attempts after Superwoman's cramping definitions of success and excellence can only place frustrating limits on your own, and you can therefore feel free to ignore her and concentrate on being something much more interesting instead, like yourself.

I have to assume, of course, that by now you don't any longer entertain any serious doubts that Superwoman really has gone on too long for your own good, or would deny in your heart that she's been conning you all along the line, but you just want to work out how she's done it and how you can get out of the mess she's got you into. She has actually done it by making one single simple mistake (and that, by the light of her burning ideal, with the best of intentions); she has signally failed to allow for the human factor in any of her equations for a perfect world. It's easily done – Adam was pretty well an after-thought, after all, never mind Eve, – but it is a rather glaring omission when her perfect world is supposed to exist through the very humans she's forgotten; it is also an omission which has almost inevitably led to dictatorship whenever it has been made before. The pursuit of a uniform society has always been abhorrent to the majority of the stubbornly diverse human race, and has always been particularly bitterly resisted in the West, where we tend to have a healthy respect for muddle and dislike of any regime that tries to tidy it up: thus Superwoman's cavalier disregard for our sacred right to make a mess of our lives all by ourselves ranges her quite definitely with the tyrants. For a woman to succeed in any one conventional thing she wanted to do in the bad old male-dominated days may have required phenomenal amounts of perseverance, talent and courage, but individual women did occasionally manage it; they had a marginally better chance of achieving their personal aims when they were simply expected not to have any than under Superwoman, who demands that yours should be the same as hers for the collective good, and who then makes any sense of fulfilment even more impossible by decreeing that if you haven't succeeded in everything – which of course you now know you can't – then you've failed in it all. I don't suppose Joan of Arc or Angelica Kaufmann was much of a hand at petit-point, or George Eliot at housekeeping; one excellence was quite enough for them, so why shouldn't it be for you? Paradoxically, therefore, it is by settling for less than Superwoman demands of you that you can actually achieve much more; by reintroducing the human factor you can take her equation beyond the stultifying formula it is for uniformity, and make the quantum leap into the far more challenging and exciting realms of individuality.

You would certainly be an unusually conformist person – and would-be Superwomen, necessarily in view of their trail-blazing activities, are rarely that – if you hadn't already succumbed to fairly regular bouts of mutiny; moments of self-mockery when you've caught yourself pursuing some more than averagely futile imperative of Superwoman's, only to wonder at yourself, in full chase, for behaving in such a patently illogical and self-destructive fashion. But myth or no, tyrant or no, Superwoman still exerts a very powerful influence over all of us; we have been well trained in our faith in her, so it is inevitably difficult for us to accept that the shining idol we have striven after for so long, and which has always hovered so tantalisingly just out of our reach, might after all have feet of clay.

Moreover, we have no new image ready to set up in her place, and to abandon a known order only to launch ourselves into the void is a step we are understandably reluctant to take. We all need role models to affirm our belief in our own rightness; to reassure ourselves that we aren't going completely out on a limb as long as our behaviour has the seal of approval endowed by its similarity to somebody else's; and Superwoman set herself up as nothing if not the role model to end all role models. Any successor we might choose to supplant her with would sooner or later reveal the same dictatorial disposition and the same inelasticity of mind as Superwoman, and would therefore ultimately be equally unsatisfactory; yet to depose her but leave her throne vacant would be to expose ourselves to the frightening possibility of relying on our own self-determined judgement – a freedom quite appallingly intimidating to the average human being, never mind to women, who have never before had the chance to test themselves in this way. And so we cling to the role model we've got, partly for fear of what might happen if we let go: we admit she sometimes goes a bit too far, but are less reluctant to accept her foibles in this than to abandon her altogether.

Not only have we no ready-made image to replace Superwoman with, but we are also only just coming to have a clear idea of what her image is. She hasn't, after all, been with us for very long, and the formative years of our allegiance to her have been spent in such an atmosphere of general social disorientation, as we shook off the ties of our former dictators, that a coherent picture of Superwoman's style of government is only now beginning to emerge. For a rebellion to gain any widespread force and currency, the rebels need to feel completely confident of what they are rebelling against; the target for disaffection must be clearly recognizable and uncompromisingly fixed. Superwoman's own revolution, against the circumscribed role of women as wives and mothers and nothing else, was made possible – and even given its success – by the very rigidity and longevity of the social structures it sought to destroy; but to rebel against Superwoman, when you are still coming to terms with what she actually is, is a much more daunting undertaking, and all the more so because you played such an honourably active part in setting her on her throne in the first place. Still battle-weary from *that* rebellion, and still half-convinced of the righteousness of the cause you had espoused, you are understandably reluctant to start rethinking your principles and beginning the battle again from scratch. And perhaps the most difficult of all obstacles to your desire for change is the problem that any revolution against Superwoman would have to be a revolution in the cause of moderation and individuality, neither of which makes a particularly rousing ideological rallying cry – and both of which open the door to distinctly alarming levels of freedom for which nothing in our lives has so far equipped us. It's hardly surprising that we bear those ills we have, rather than flying to such frighteningly limitless possibilities.

Yet despite the difficulties of gearing ourselves up to it, the rebellion has already begun, though it has so far stopped short of anything more forceful than mutinous mutterings. The mutterings have been going on for some time now among the grass roots of womankind, and are starting to gain currency with a handful of more strategically placed malcontents: the idea that Superwoman has outlived her usefulness is rapidly catching on. In the autumn of 1983, the *Sunday Times* saw the need for a new role model when it asked its readers (or the readers of its so-called women's pages, anyway) 'Who is "the *Sunday*

*Times* woman"?'; *Woman's Journal* set out on a similar voyage of discovery in March 1984 with 'Are you a *Woman's Journal* woman?'; Jill Tweedie's *Fainthearted Feminist*, Betty Friedan's *Second Stage* and Germaine Greer's *Sex and Destiny* had already, in their very different ways, responded to particular facets of Superwoman's tyranny over us. And in February 1984 the *Guardian* ran a week of enquiry into 'Who is the Ideal Woman? And is She to be Encouraged?', in the course of which Polly Toynbee came out and named names in open defiance: 'Dud Ideal Women are strewn in our path at regular intervals – and Shirley Conran's Superwoman is one of the worst offenders. She is not only Earth Mother, but also Liberated Career Woman, Mistress and Hostess too . . . Selling this Ideal Woman has made super-liberated Shirley Conran millions, and millions of women miserable.'

So you see there is nothing earthshatteringly innovative in the desire to be rid of her – though it is interesting to note that in most cases a new candidate is still being sought for the post of heroine. 'The Queen is dead, long live the Queen' is a structured change which we can easily accept or even embrace; 'The Queen is dead, there will be no more queens' is an iconoclasm we aren't yet entirely ready to brave. Yet an empty throne, if we could find the courage to face it, offers exactly the sort of freedom that we are now readier for than we realize; it threatens anarchy only inasmuch as it is anarchy to encompass in one society all the diversity of aims and aspirations, talents and weaknesses, principles and compromises, that make up the human factor Superwoman so brutally left out. And we wouldn't have to abandon our role models completely, either – we will still always need or want the encouragement of the exceptional in single areas of behaviour and achievement. All we would have to do would be to assert ourselves enough to announce that we no longer require one single, sterile, universal role model to dictate all things to all women. As the dust of the past two decades of social flux and wing-stretching begins to settle, women are becoming more and more confident of our individual bases of existence, and readier to go beyond the rule books to place our faith in ourselves. Even such minor revolutions as wearing a scarlet shirt to the office, or leaving the washing-up for tomorrow, are a step in the right direction and give a remarkably heady sense of liberty: just consider what horizons will stretch before you once you discover that you are more than ready to slough off the rest of Superwoman's all-pervasive and constricting dogma, and open yourself to the long-forgotten luxury of the more satisfying pursuit of personal happiness!

Which sounds like just as impossible a miracle cure as anything Superwoman ever told you, and rather more selfish. Yet happiness is such an extremely simple, and very basic, human desire that we're sometimes in danger of forgetting about it altogether, or dismissing it, as Superwoman does, as less basic than base; and one of the most damaging aspects of the Superwoman Trap is that it really *does* make 'millions of women miserable'. Who could avoid being miserable, when every action she undertakes is represented to her as a long, hard grind in which anything less than perfection is wanton failure? In a world where going to a party is regarded as on par with fighting a war; sex as an Olympic sport; doing the job you love an unworthy goal unless you are carving your way through it for the ultimate benefit of generations yet unborn; motherhood as a moralistic minefield rather than a rewarding experience? What room has Superwoman left for the simple (and to her, no doubt, disconcerting) fact that you might just possibly prefer to get on with your own life in your own way rather than to get through it better and faster? What latitude is there in the ranks of her model army for the idea that you might conceivably be more important and more interesting as the separate parts than as the whole, or that – unlike school sports – you don't have to compete if you don't want to? Of course you're miserable. And for Superwoman to have the sheer cheek to offer you happiness as a reward for success in something where you can never achieve success, thereby morally blackmailing you into accepting misery as your inevitable and deserved fate as the penalty for failure, should be enough to cause all women to rise in their miserable millions forthwith and not just depose but murder the arrogant bitch.

Not, of course, that you're likely to do any such thing, especially not while you are still under the effects of her training – and not, of course, that you would gain anything more than a transient moment of satisfaction if you did. But the damage she has done to the happiness of a whole generation of women, to the self-confidence she promised (and, to be fair, believed) she was building up, is nonetheless such a serious offence that you at least can't continue to connive at it. So what, since you have quite obviously got to do something to rid yourself of her domination, can you do?

At the very least, recognizing the Superwoman Trap as existing gives you a nice neat label for the confusing and contradictory continuum of impossible aims and unhappy effort which you thought were doomed to be your normal way of life. Labels can be very useful for relieving yourself of responsibility and for soaking up blame. Just as 'I've got 'flu' sounds more reassuringly like the fault of an outside agency which can't possibly be laid at your door than does 'I don't feel well', so 'I'm in the Superwoman Trap' takes your failure to be Superwoman right out of your hands, endows your miseries and inadequacies with an external cause totally unconnected with any shortcomings of your own, and places the blame fairly and squarely back on Superwoman for creating the trap in the first place. This may sound feebly like opting out to you, but the responsibility for not being Superwoman is one which you can and should relinquish at the earliest opportunity without being too fussy about how: your new freedom will bring you plenty of others to replace it with, and rather more constructive ones at that. Besides, anyone starting on the slow crawl out of the Superwoman Trap and back into the human race deserves to indulge in a little feebleness along the way.

The simplest and most obvious way out of the Trap starts with being aware that it's there – and if you've got this far through the catalogue of classic Trap situations your antennae should have picked it up pretty clearly by now. Once you've come to terms with the idea that you aren't going to be Superwoman, then even if you can't quite mentally strip her of all the glitter of heroism you can at least relieve yourself of some of the pressure you impose on yourself to try so hard to emulate her. If you once admit openly that the aim is impossible in any case, you can stop torturing yourself with a crushing and destructive burden of guilt at not having achieved it – because nobody in her right mind can possibly feel guilty for failing to attain the unattainable or perform miracles twenty-four hours a day, seven days a week. (I know you *can*, and I know that you still can even when you have accepted that you're on a complete no-hoper and know perfectly well that you are indulging in dangerous folly: but you are going to change all that.) It is a strange but comforting truth that the second step towards freedom from guilt is as easy as the first is difficult: once you delegate the painting of the sitting-room, it's that much simpler to delegate the making of the curtains as well; when you have once sent an extra curricular job to the rightabout you can do it twice (or may even be lucky enough to find that it doesn't try it on a second time anyway). Every little bit of guilt shed gives you more freedom to deviate from the prescribed path of Superwomanhood, until before you know it you really will be a human being again. It's guilt, rather than genuine loyalty, that keeps you tied to Superwoman's apron strings: guilt which makes you overstressed and unhappy, and then – because stress and misery are your punishment for not trying hard enough – guilty . . .

Although it doesn't necessarily stop you feeling guilty all at once – and you can even manage, if you're well and truly trapped, to feel guilty at the same time – catching yourself out in Trap attitudes and actions and laughing at yourself for it is extraordinarily therapeutic. Try it some time – like now, instead of sighing impatiently that it's all very well for me to talk; it's surprisingly liberating to stand back for a moment and see just how silly you can be. When you wonder at yourself for chasing so diligently after Superwoman's will o' the wisps, don't stop at wondering, but laugh: nobody with a real sense of the absurd can remain in the Superwoman Trap for long, since it is such a ripe field for absurdity. Besides which, as long as you're being gloomily puritanical about your life in approved Superwoman style, nobody will dare to distract you from its weighty concerns with any frivolous, irresponsible suggestions of relaxing, so you'll get no help in going back to being human again: but a lively sense of the ridiculous is a characteristic so infinitely more attractive than a model figure or a dedicated assiduity in the accounts that if you foster yours you could quite easily find that your social life expands so rapidly you simply don't have time to get paranoid about the cobwebs on the hall ceiling any more. Of such small sillinesses are neuroses made and broken.

One of the silliest things about the Superwoman Trap is the way you spot it instantly as it yawns before others, but never before yourself. You will be perfectly prepared to spend hours lecturing a friend or colleague severely, for her own good, about going home on time, or getting someone in to paper the bathroom, or the complete lack of necessity for tomato chutney, yet find nothing inconsistent in leaving her, glowing with virtue, only to return to your own crazy goals with exactly the same manic vigour that you were trying to talk her out of. Nor, even as you issue her with your stern warning about stress, will you fail to feel obscurely cheated and let down if she doesn't then work until midnight to finish a job that you consider important, which is very illogical of you indeed. You know as you do it that it's absurd, but you keep right on doing it anyway, and that really *is* absurd: in fact it's so ridiculous that you ought by rights to set out and have yourself certified immediately. What's more, the absurdity works for other women as well, as you might remember next time you think of succumbing to peer-group pressure that will drive you deeper into the Trap: the other women who are pushing you into it are only doing so because they are in it themselves and have mistaken the inner reaches for the way out, and besides, it makes them feel less guiltily inadequate if they can crack the whip over a woman less trapped than themselves. Which is only all the more reason to topple Superwoman once and for all, before we have got ourselves too tangled up to be able to.

Even if you can't quite find your behaviour funny enough to allow you to abandon whatever Supermountain you're climbing forthwith, only a very little sense of humour will at least allow you to approach it in an altogether lighter vein. Not only is this a whole lot better for you but oddly enough it's quite often considerably better for the job in hand as well: you stand a much higher chance of botching something completely if you set about it too earnestly, and with too much doom-laden conviction of the importance of getting it right than if you can step a little away from it and give yourself a clearer overall picture of what's required. And if you do make a mistake, you've made a mistake: they do happen, even to the best regulated of people. Unless you actually press the big red button or carelessly cook the baby, it isn't the end of the world, but in fact occasionally even has its funny aspects, and the day you learn to see that it is the day you can start being genuinely optimistic about the chances of life after Superwoman.

Nobody can do everything, and you certainly can't do everything perfectly all of the time, especially not when you're trying to do so much of it at once: so now we've got that clear, you can make some practical moves to stop. The major change you need to make – and I admit it's easier said than done – is to set your standards a fraction below perfection, take a long, clear look at your priorities, and cultivate the art of the possible. If it is more important to meet a deadline than to come up with a prize-winning design, then there's no point agonizing over shortcomings probably imperceptible to anyone but you; you can win the prize another time, when you have relaxed enough to stop worrying about a deadline that isn't really dead. If your career is more important to you than your decor, you don't have to repaint the hall; if you can't make pastry, you don't have to cook pies; if a nappy needs changing, dusting the mantelpiece will have to wait and if you haven't had time to varnish your nails you can wow Him with the new natural look instead. You know what matters most to you – and it's your life, not Superwoman's. *You* also know what you can do; you don't have to keep proving it to anyone else. Rather, extend your self-knowledge by recognizing, without apportioning blame, that there are also things you *can't* do. And while you will no doubt continue to apply the most exacting standards to yourself, you should temper your self-criticism with an occasional silent litany of self-praise; we all need the carrot as well as the stick, and the idea that you should never admit to anything but bad of yourself is a good deal older than Superwoman but every bit as harshly puritanical – Superwoman just made it easier for you to justify.

A word of warning, though: the first heady taste of freedom from perfection can send you off the rails completely, and lead you to deny that you can do anything at all, so beware, in case you turn into one of those hideous 'poor little me' women who seem to be incapable of doing more than fluttering an eyelash without the help of outside – preferably male – agencies. You know them, and you would heartily despise yourself for turning into one of them, so before you admit to your areas of incompetence be sure that they really are areas of incompetence rather than inertia. There is no more reason, for example, why you should be incapable of unjamming the photocopier than of unblocking the sink, which you wouldn't think twice about if you needed to; but if you talk too loudly and too often about how terrible you are at sewing, say, then the day you think you would actually rather like to embark on haute couture you could well find that you have closed your mind so firmly against the possibility that you daren't even set about learning. Strike a balance, then, between admitting what you can't do and reminding yourself of what you can: as long as there's a comforting preponderance of pluses over minuses (and there almost certainly will be unless you're so trapped you're cheating against yourself) you will be able to accept your shortcomings without having to despise yourself for them.

Wherever possible – which means outside paid employment, but virtually everywhere else – get into the habit of paying people to do for you the things that need to be done, and especially the things that cause your acutest anxiety attacks, whether that means something major like decorating or servicing the car or minor, like ironing. You aren't being lazy; you've got more than enough to do, or you wouldn't even be contemplating such an unSuperwomanlike step. Nor need you worry about compromising your egalitarian principles – it's not as if you are planning to employ a staff of ten to look after one little you and be treated as inferiors for their pains. All you are doing is recognizing the professionalism of the worker you employ, and at the same time providing much-needed employment in an age when the dignity of work is a considerably more sought-after commodity than any freedom from the servitude of earning one's keep – so you could even indulge in a small twinge of virtue at doing your bit to counter unemployment. (But only a very small twinge: I suspect that Lady Bountiful was just as unpleasant in her way as Scrooge was in his.) If money is a problem – and when isn't it? – do, once more, be sure whether it is a real problem or a perceived one before you reject the idea out of hand as impossibly extravagant: there's no point at all in being at ease with your bank manager at the expense of being at ease with yourself, or in saving for your old age if you're killing yourself through overwork and general stress before you ever get there.

When you come to the boring daily round of chores that really can't sensibly be done by anyone but you (you *are* making sure that everyone in your household is already taking an equal share in them, aren't you?), first of all consider whether they need to be done at all: a number of things don't. Unanswered letters quite often end up dealing with themselves; if you left the bed unmade this morning, there's not an awful lot of point making it an hour before you get back into it unless you do so simply because you find it more comfortable to sleep in that way, and for no reason connected with appearances or duty at all; that blessed tomato chutney isn't an essential life-enhancement at all. And if the jobs do need to be done, do they need to be done now? Will your world collapse around you if the washing-up waits until tomorrow, or the curtains go for their annual spree to the cleaners in the summer rather than the spring? And *why* do these jobs need to be done: how much does it matter to you if there's a button missing from your shirt (depending, of course, on which button), or your dinner guests are faced by a choice between only two puddings? '*Hang* spring cleaning!' cried Mole in exasperation, as he set off to follow his inclinations rather than his duty – and look what happened to him. The residue of tedium that does have to be got through will be a lot easier to face (and there'll be a lot less of it) if you aren't permanently bowed down by the attempt to make it fill your whole life, but are ready to down tools whenever the river beckons on a warm spring day: leaven is necessary to every dough, and variety to every performance.

Odd as it may sound, it is actually a good idea to grumble to your friends about your lot – though not, please, to the boring exclusion of any other topic of conversation. A good moan is not only an excellent safety valve, releasing whole gouts of tension and temper in a safety-controlled way, but if you listen to yourself retailing in high indignation the latest drama or imposition, and can't see the humour of it, then you're nearly past praying for. But as long as your friends are there they'll see the joke even if you don't, just as you will when you listen sympathetically in your turn to their complaints about their lives. And of course you will listen to them, since you know that self-obsession is both extremely uninteresting and a classic symptom of the Trap-ee: they're probably just as trapped as you are anyway, so give them a turn. Besides, you can't afford to lose them over anything as silly as your Superwomanly ambitions, since you'll need them around later on for when you spring the trap and embark on your social life again . . .

There is a strict limit to how far practical solutions can take you on your route out of the Trap, since the minute they go one step too far they tend to harden into formulae, so you would find that you were merely replacing one rule-book with another, which would be rather defeating the object. The whole reason for Superwoman becoming a tyrant in the first place was that she operated a set of rules, imposed on us from the outside, which petrified – there is therefore no future in setting up a new version of the same system just by changing the wording slightly. If it's rules you want, take your copy of *Superwoman* (but do yourself a favour and cross out the more hyperactive bits): you've had all you're going to get from me.

Unfortunately, because there is no code of conduct on offer on the far side of the Superwoman Trap there can also be no cut-and-dried answers to its dilemmas. Out in the real world there aren't the confines of spurious rules and black-and-white solutions; if that's where you want to live, then you have to accept that you are one of myriads of individual worries with individual problems and priorities, and are entitled to your own highly individual ways of working them out however suits you best. Women have not had the easiest of rides over the past few centuries, but that's all the more reason to stop the Superworld and get off. As your self-confidence increases daily, you will find that your own approval is a much sounder basis for your actions than is anyone else's; that you have more interesting and potentially more rewarding things to do with your time and energy than to waste them on competing with a myth. I'm sorry if that sounds too vague and idealistic for anyone brought up on Superwoman's passion for detail and duty, but if so it's only because it's so blindingly obvious that we tend to overlook it: like the purloined letter, the human factor you were missing was actually there all the time – in you, and you, and you . . .

Of course we will still continue to crave the approval of 'society' – whether that means our peers, our mothers, our men, our children, Superwoman or anyone else who happens to put a toe into our universe. Of course life will go on being irritating, and boring, and demanding; of course we will go on setting impossible standards for ourselves, and so will other people for us; of course we will go on alternating between rebellion and conformity, delirious happiness and deepest gloom, confidence and paranoia; and of course we won't stop feeling guilty or doubtful of ourselves just for telling ourselves not to. But we're out of school now, and we can perfectly well contrive all these follies on our own account, without having to be bullied into them by a jumped-up prefect with an impressive title. And the confidence you find in yourself will be stronger than any gleaned from others; win your own approval and the approval of your peers will follow. And if you must be guilty – as you almost certainly sometimes must – turn it to a virtue and be, like Christopher Fry's countess in *The Dark is Light Enough*, 'always perfectly guilty of what I do/Thank God.'

And look over your shoulder to watch Superwoman disappearing up her own trap, and wonder mildly how you ever fell for it.

**MEGATRENDS**

**Ten new directions transforming our lives**

**by John Naisbitt**

Using techniques of newspaper analysis first devised in World War II, John Naisbitt looks at ten trends observable in today's world and predicts the developments of the future. A primer for the eighties that shows just where our sophisticated technology is taking us, he points to the shifts from industrial society to information society, from centralization to decentralization, from institutional help to self-help and advises us how we can adapt to and capitalize on them.

'John Naisbitt is one of the shrewdest observers of the changes sweeping America today' Alvin Toffler, author of FUTURE SHOCK

'A thoughtful work which makes a plea for technology on a human scale' *The Guardian*

Futura Publications
Non-Fiction
0 7088 2508 7

**PAPER MONEY**

**Adam Smith**

We live in an anxious era: confusion in the money markets, increasing unemployment, unease about interest rates and the money supply. We feel things may be skidding out of control.

Adam Smith, author of THE MONEY GAME and SUPERMONEY now turns his unique combination of literary and financial talent to an explanation of how it all happened and what happens next. With wit and intelligence he describes how property values, OPEC, oil prices, the energy crisis, the stock market and the financial world as a whole, tie-in with inflation and the chilling vision of the 'wheel barrow full of money'.

Futura Publications
Non-Fiction
0 7088 2163 4

**DANGER! MEN AT WORK**

**Rosalind Miles**

HOW TO MAKE IT IN A MAN'S WORLD

So you think the battle for sexual equality is over and won? That new laws have made the workplace a paradise of female opportunity? Think again!

It's more like a jungle where you're in constant danger from hostile natives, and likely to experience

★ SEXUAL HARASSMENT
★ DELIBERATE DISCRIMINATION
★ LACK OF TRAINING
★ BARRIERS TO PROMOTION

But don't despair! The wind of change is blowing up the trouserlegs of the male powerholders. Women everywhere are taking a long cool look at their situation and refusing to accept the status quo. And here is a vital handbook to help you on the way.

Wise, witty, well-informed, often irreverent, always positive – this is the indispensable guide through the minefield of the workplace.

So get out there and at 'em – you've nothing to lose but your chains.

Futura Publications
Non-fiction/General
0 7088 2371 8